# Marketing Practice in the Hotel and Catering Industry

## ——— John W Shepherd ———

BA, ACMA, Dip. in M, M Inst. M, Dip. IAM
Principal Lecturer, Hollings Faculty,
Manchester Polytechnic

B T BATSFORD LIMITED   LONDON

© John W Shepherd 1982
First published 1982
Reprinted 1985
Reprinted 1987

Typeset by Tek-Art Ltd, Kent
and printed in Great Britain by
Billing & Son Ltd
London, Guildford & Worcester
for the publishers
B T Batsford Ltd
4 Fitzhardinge Street
London W1H 0AH

ISBN 0 7134 0498 1

# Contents

# Acknowledgment

I would like to acknowledge the help given by colleagues who supported the preparation of this book, in particular:

Dr G Wilson for the initial encouragement and time off to visit hotels and catering firms.

Miss B Hollingshead and D M Yorke at the Education Methods Unit, Manchester Polytechnic, for their many useful suggestions.

D Pugh and the many students who, while at Hollings Faculty, have worked with me on the hotel and catering projects which are recorded in this book.

The HCIMA for granting permission for me to include past examination questions.

Brian Quarmby of South Devon Technical College for having read the draft manuscript and given his valuable comments.

Jean, Madeline and Beryl who did most of the typing.

My wife, Sylvia, for her constant help in the presentation of the book.

*Manchester 1982*                                                    JWS

---

**Readings**

For further study the student is referred to:

GILES , G B, *Marketing*, Macdonald and Evans Handbooks, 1980

KOTAS, RICHARD (editor), *Market Orientation*, Surrey University Press, 1975

# Introduction

This book has been written for students studying for the new TEC Higher and Ordinary Diploma, and those taking degree courses directed towards the hotel and catering industry, also employees who have a managerial responsibility for operating a catering unit and who wish to familiarise themselves with, and acquire the practical skills of marketing.

The basic principles of marketing and their relationship to the hotel and catering industry are dealt with as a link to the books written about marketing generally. The main purpose of this text is to present, through inter-related case studies, activities, and projects, an insight of how managers apply the principles of marketing in practice.

Managers within the hotel and catering industry use marketing as a tool to integrate the operational areas to achieve optimum profitability and consumer satisfaction. Consequently, emphasis is placed on financial and behavioural aspects.

The worked examples and case studies are taken from the industry and by working through them the student should:

1 obtain a knowledge and understanding of marketing principles and their application to the industry, and
2 develop the ability to analyse, identify, interpret and present information in qualitative and quantitative terms, which will lead him to make decisions after sound and effective judgement.

The cases and activities have been applied to a fictitious hotel to enable the essential aspects of marketing to be related and integrated in the mind of the reader.

# I
# Introduction to Marketing

**Areas of study**
1 Marketing and selling
2 Social changes leading to consumer orientation
3 The meaning of the marketing concept to the hotel and catering industry
4 The application of marketing to the hotel and catering industry
5 The marketing concept applied to institutional and welfare sections of the industry

**Objectives**
On completing this chapter the reader should be able to:
(a) define the concept of marketing orientation
(b) explain the basic role of marketing within the hotel and catering industry
(c) identify the social changes leading to market orientation
(d) describe the factors included within a marketing system

**Activities**
1 Multiple choice questions on the marketing concept
2 Self-assessment questions
3 Test I

**Readings**
GILES , *Marketing*, Chapter 1

## 1 Marketing and selling

The Hotel and catering industry has for many years assumed that customers will respond to, and be satisfied by, a well produced and correctly priced product, flavoured by social skills and a dash of atmosphere; and to make a profit, the management has been orientated towards selling sufficient products and services.

*Diagram of the production and selling process*

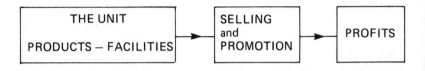

Whilst production and selling orientation has been successful for many catering organisations in the past, society has now developed towards a stage where consumer or market orientation is essential for the future.

The 1960s saw customers' needs, wants, expectations and desires grow tremendously while at the same time increase in investment capital, and new technology made it easy to change and react quickly to market demand. The customer has become the generating force for change and innovation in the catering industry and, in fact, in all our industries because of the social changes during the last two decades.

## 2 Social changes, leading to consumer orientation

The social changes during the last two decades have reduced the restrictions on the consumer so that he is able to express his wishes and choose, and change, his wants more frequently in a discriminating way because of:

(a) the increase in salaried staffs and jobs providing more disposable incomes
(b) rising standards of education, cultural activities and hobbies
(c) a better informed and more persuasive media industry
(d) improved means of transportation enabling more people to travel abroad and return with new wants and desires
(e) increased leisure time for holidays and week-ends.

Consequently, businessmen and industrialists have found that success is more likely to come from being able to carry out the MARKETING PROCESS of:

(a) anticipating and assessing customers wants and desires
(b) adapting the product, facilities and services to satisfy customers

10

(c) persuading customers to visit and consume products, facilities and services
(d) controlling events to produce mutual benefits to both producer and consumer.

*The diagram shows that production and selling have now become part of the marketing process which starts and ends with considering the* CONSUMER.

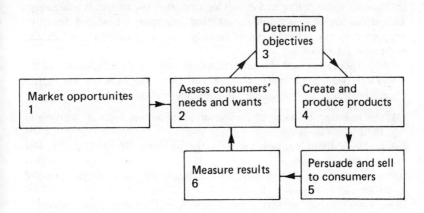

**The marketing process**

**Activity**

Write down the main factors which have influenced the change from production — selling orientation to consumer-market orientation:

1 _____

2 _____

3 _____

4 _____

## 3 The meaning of the marketing concept in the hotel and catering industry

Marketing has been described as a philosophy directing the attitudes and objectives of a business. It is that energy, thought, decision and action taken by every person in a business, must be made after considering their customers.

We could react by suggesting that caterers and hoteliers have always had a direct and close relationship with their customers, so what else does marketing offer to the industry?

Perhaps the answer lies in the definition made by the Institute of Marketing, 'that marketing is the management process, responsible for identifying, anticipating and satisfying customer requirements profitably'. This definition suggests that 'marketing is a series of related activities, supported by the effective use of techniques, to give customer satisfaction and profit for a business'.

Whilst accepting that the definition above gives a good indication of the marketing process generally, the hotel and catering industry has certain characteristics which we should take into account, namely:

(a) the industry is made of thousands of individual units all working to their own objectives
(b) there is direct contact between the producer of goods and service and the consumer
(c) the importance of successful personal interaction between the manager/staff and customers
(d) a catering unit can have several markets — lunch-time guests can differ from evening guests, and the summer guests may be tourists, the winter guests businessmen.

Consequently a better definition of Marketing for the Hotel and Catering Industry would be.

Marketing is the management process which establishes an operating policy for a company or individual unit, which organises all those business activities involved in ascertaining, creating and satisfying customer needs and wants to the mutual benefit of producer and consumer.

The main factors contained within a marketing system for a catering unit can be divided into four areas:

(i) Consumer orientation
(ii) Marketing research
(iii) Marketing planning
(iv) Marketing control

### (i) Consumer orientation
This is:
(a) an attempt to understand buyer behaviour by ascertaining:

(i) past and present 'needs' and 'wants' and
(ii) what motivates and changes opinions and purchasing decisions

(b) the study of environmental aspects which can help to highlight changes and opportunities in the future.

### (ii) Marketing research
This is the systematic collection recording and analysis of data related to factors bearing on a business operation in an attempt to improve the efficiency and effectiveness of supply and demand.

(a) Demand is assessed by a market analysis, which identifies consumers and their needs and wants
(b) Supply is analysed by a product analysis which determines the strengths and weaknessess of a unit compared with competitors
(c) While a financial and statistical analysis will highlight areas needing attention or development.

### (iii) Marketing planning
From marketing research data, objectives, policy and plans can be developed to relate to the:

> product
> place
> promotion
> people
> profitability

### (iv) Marketing control
Control must seek to ensure that the objectives are likely to be achieved and highlight any change that might be necessary.
The two main areas are.

1   customer satisfaction rates
2   financial results

*The four main aspects link together to form a system which is continually adjusted as changes and innovations are made in the market and the products.*

*A Marketing system for a catering unit*

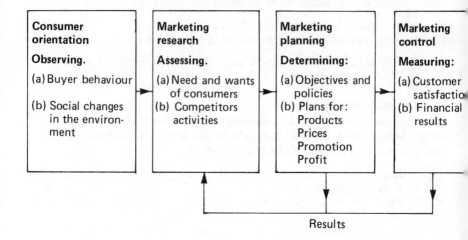

| Consumer orientation | Marketing research | Marketing planning | Marketing control |
|---|---|---|---|
| **Observing.** | **Assessing.** | **Determining:** | **Measuring:** |
| (a) Buyer behaviour | (a) Need and wants of consumers | (a) Objectives and policies | (a) Customer satisfaction |
| (b) Social changes in the environment | (b) Competitors activities | (b) Plans for: Products Prices Promotion Profit | (b) Financial results |

Results

## 4 The application of marketing to the hotel and catering industry

In applying the marketing concept to a catering unit we must:

(a) become customer orientated, and
(b) integrate operations to satisfy the customers and meet objectives.

This means the development of a system of operations which will establish marketing opportunities and operating procedures, integrating and guiding all departments and levels of management. See diagram above.

**Note**
The book is presented to follow the model shown above.

## 5 The marketing concept applied to institutional and welfare sectors of the industry

Though the market process is mainly linked with the commercial side of the Industry we must remember that many organisations within the non-profit making sector of the industry, usually catering for a captive market, are becoming more consumer orientated.

They have appreciated that by heightening the meal experience, through improved presentation, choice of meals, different services and generally reacting to satisfy consumers wants and needs:

— waste can be reduced
— social benefits can be provided
— consumer satisfaction can be increased.

14

The consumer in the captive market can obtain increased satisfaction from being able to:

— select fruit from a basket
— smell coffee being served
— see colourful items on a plate
— read a well presented menu
— determine the nutritional value of items for weight watching, etc
— select from different services — pub grub, grills or snacks

It is interesting to note that after procedures for forecasting sales and assessing patient opinions were introduced by the Group Catering Manager of Kings College Hospital food costs decreased by 10% for the year although patient population increased by 2%. Patient satisfaction levels increased and waste was reduced from 300 grammes per patient a day to 185 grammes per patient a day. (A copy of a Patient Opinion Survey is included on page 53, *Marketing Research*)

# Activities

## 1 Multiple choice questions The marketing concept

From the following statements choose what you consider to be the correct answers.

1 The basic function of a manager working for a market orientated catering firm is:
(a)  to increase sales
(b)  to utilize all the factors of production
(c)  to supply goods and services which satisfy consumer needs
(d)  to buy the latest products and technical equipment.

2 Which one of the following statements best describes a market orientated approach:
(a)  products and services should be the best possible
(b)  products and services should be designed to meet what the potential consumer is prepared to pay
(c)  products and services well promoted, presented and priced will find a market
(d)  products and services should be designed to satisfy customers needs and wants and provide a profit.

3   A major long term benefit from adopting a market orientated approach is that:
(a)  better products are produced
(b)  increased sales lead to greater profits
(c)  products are designed to satisfy consumers
(d)  costs are reduced.

4   The following factors have led to the consumer being more influential and firms adopting the marketing concept, except:
(a)  increased disposable income
(b)  increased information, education and publicity
(c)  increased competition
(d)  increased mobility
(e)  increased leisure time.

## 2   Self-assessment questions

After working through the study material and text books test your knowledge by:

1   Identifying the social changes leading to market orientation.
2   Defining marketing.
3   Describing the difference between 'marketing' and 'selling'.
4   Defining the concept of marketing orientation.

## 3   Test I

1   Increasing emphasis is being placed on marketing within the hotel and catering industry.
   Discuss the reasons for this, relating your answer to both the profit and the welfare sectors of the industry.

2   Describe the various management activities comprising the 'marketing function'.

# II
# Consumer Orientation

**Areas of study**
1  Introduction to consumer orientation
2  Market segmentation
3  Understanding the consumer
4  Environmental and social changes
5  Stages in a buying decision

**Objectives**
On completing this chapter the reader should be able to:
(a)  identify the most important environmental factors influencing the consumer
(b)  define market segmentation
(c)  explain and describe the main factors influencing a buying decision
(d)  describe the stages in a buying decision

**Activities**
1  Identifying the factors that influence a person when choosing a restaurant
2  Self-assessment questions
3  Test II

**Readings**
GILES, *Marketing*, Chapter II,

# 1 Introduction to consumer orientation

Consumer needs vary and fluctuate from day to day according to the situation they find themselves in, shopping, entertaining, on business etc. Consequently a catering establishment has to direct its operation to a mixture of 'market segments' and 'market needs', which can be identified as:

(a) the captive food market
(b) the mass food market
(c) the self-expressive food market
(d) the status food market

### (a) The captive food market

Hospitals patients and families with lean budgets consume food with the conscious need to survive uppermost in their minds. While flight catering operations, school meal organisers and hospitals must consider the serving of food linking it with security needs. A young child at school needs to feel secure during the lunch, which is achieved by providing a family service with eight children to a table, headed by someone who can develop social training — correct use of cutlery. Similar factors are considered in hospitals with group eating and to a lesser extent in flight catering and industrial canteens.

### (b) The mass food market

This market is the largest and most changeable and consequently the most competitive. Sandwich bars, pub-grub, transport cafeterieas and small general restaurants supply the need to obtain quick, inexpensive food.

### (c) The self-expressive food market

More and more people are seeking a meal experience in pleasant and distinctive surroundings with a fast service often supported by wine. These speciality restaurants reflect the need to renew experiences and memories from visits abroad and the desire to seek change. These catering units place more emphasis on the main course, make the use of prepared foods, to reduce labour costs, stock levels, and fuel usuage. This is reflected in the growth of carveries, pizza bars, Italian and French bistros and units supported by extensive merchandising.

### (d) The status food market

This market embraces restaurants which are highly regarded by people, the clientele being affluent, well-dressed, and symbolising success to themselves and others.

These four categories basically reflect demand and needs within the total market.

A unit manager will use market segmentation to become consumer orientated, as it recognises the need to pinpoint the sections of the market in which to operate.

## 2 Market segmentation

The Hotel and catering industry has been described by Professor Medlik as the economic activity of undertakings which aim to satisfy demand for accommodation, food and drink away from home.

The demand constitutes the total market for the hotel and catering services. But it consists of the sum of the demands made by each market segment or submarket containing people who have the same needs, wants and ability to pay to fulfil them.

Market segmentation is the process of dividing the total market into segments. The most frequently used classification by company or unit managers are ones that are measurable and accessible. Examples are given below:

1  social-economic, including details of sex, age, income levels, education and occupation
2  product-related, customer groups which are identified according to a product purchased, such as a newspaper or by belonging to a professional body eg The Institute of Marketing
3  usership segments, light, frequent and heavy users of catering facilities and services, linked to the reasons for being away from home
   — businessmen, tourists, local residents, conferences, transient customers

According to R Doswell in his book, *Hotel Planning*, 'the hotel market is primarily composed of four segments and that there are correspondingly four basic market packages: upper; upper/middle; middle; and lower'.

This classification can be related to economic and sociological data, based on income and occupation which is already available from many government and commercial publications.

### The advantages of market segmentation

A unit manager will find it advantageous to analyse his market into market segments so he can direct his marketing efforts towards potential customers needing and wanting part or all of the package being offered:

— location
— image
— prices
— facilities
— services
— food and accommodation

1  Prices can be made to suit particular segments, children and old age pensioners can be offered special rates.
2  Promotional campaign and messages can be designed and directed to specific types of users thus increasing effectiveness and reducing total costs. Businessmen who attend conferences

19

3 Resources can be directed to the most profitable market. Tourists from Germany will often spend more per head than other continental visitors

4 Facilities and services can be matched to market needs. Coffee-making machines for families, car-parking facilities for intransient guests

## 3 Understanding the consumer

The consumer today is able to determine what he needs and wants because he has.

(a) more wealth at his disposal
(b) better information, through increased educational facilities and improved methods of persuasive communications

The producers of goods and services therefore have to be guided not only by what the consumers need and want now, but, what they are likely to need and want in the future.

The understanding of customer behaviour usually takes two forms:

1 The study of environmental influences such as cultural, economic and sociological factors as they determine the shape and the nature of individual needs and wants

2 The process of decision making, the identification of a need, the pre-buying activity, the decision and the evaluation process.

## 4 Environmental and social changes

The hotel and catering industry was once defined as the industry that looks after people when they are away from home, and it is from this close and direct contact with its customers that caterers are more conscious than most of the continual changes in behaviour.

These changes have been caused by:

(a) the rapid advance in technology, which is changing what people can do
(b) new values and life styles, which determine what people will accept.

Many organisations are well informed of the technological changes, but as one becomes more consumer orientated more time could be profitably spent in examining changes in behaviour patterns to assist us to forecast demand, and develop products accordingly.

### Social changes
No individual is born with a set of values, standards, or ideas on how to behave or what to expect. They are learned from the family, friends, schools, churches, television and other experiences. Consequently, as contacts and experiences change and differ, so will buyer behaviour patterns. It is beyond the scope of the book to look at sociological, cultural, psychological and economic changes in detail, but, as caterers, we should be able to identify changes likely to affect the industry.

20

One of the most valuable sources of information for identifying changes is the publication — *Social Trends*, published each year by the Government Statistical Service.

Four changes are picked out as affecting the hotel and catering industry over the past 20 years.

1   Opportunities for young people have opened up. More stay on at school and go on to further and higher education, can afford to take part in leisure activities, and possess valuables at increasingly early stages
2   Workers now have more paid holidays and work fewer hours, thus having more time for leisure activities
3   Many more married women go out to work, increasing the family income
4   More British people are taking holidays in this country each year and at the same time we are receiving more visitors from overseas countries

The social changes resulting in smaller households, more married women working increased disposable income and more leisure time have all had the effect of increasing the demand for hotel and catering services and will continue into the 1980s.

The demand has not been for the traditional services and standards. During the sixties and seventies, the newly created consumer seems to prefer  to eat and drink in establishments providing an emphasis on presentation in the form of decor, atmosphere, service and in some cases entertainment.

The 1980s will be one of continued growth but the emphasis could change. The new consumers are encouraged to be price conscious, and more discriminating in the nutritional value of food to improve their appearance and health. Perhaps health food establishments, sandwich and salad bars will grow as they meet the desires of the new public and the need to reduce staff costs.

Even in the drink trade it is noticeable that the lighter coloured drinks of vodka, lager, white wines and their association with purety are increasing their sales at the expense of the darker coloured drinks.

It is by understanding the social changes that we can forecast future needs and wants and use the right technology to provide profit and satisfaction.

*Marketing and its environment*

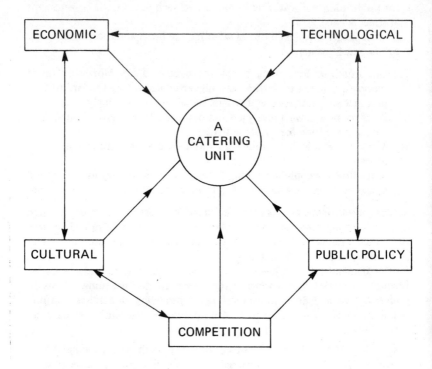

## Environmental factors
The environmental changes which influence the market, but cannot be controlled by the manager are:

(a) economic
(b) technological
(c) public policies
(d) competition
(e) cultural

Consider the effect of the following changes on a catering establish ment

(a) Economic changes
    — variations in disposable wealth
    — variations in the local population
    -- increased leisure time

(b) Technological changes
    — new materials as a substitute for meat
    — micro-wave ovens and cook chill methods
    - computers

*Continued*

- — improved transportation, motorways, jet aircraft
- — improved methods of communication
- — television, colour magazines

(c) Public policies
- — VAT increase
- — fire precautions increased
- — consumer protection laws

(c) Competition
- — overseas package holdiays
- — increased use of caravans and tents

(d) Cultural changes
- — growth of education
- — the growing freedom for women
- — the increase in the use of credit facilities

## Conclusion

Managers must accept changes as inevitable and by knowing and understanding environmental changes it can help them make right decisions to fulfil their customers' expectations.

## Consumer orientation

A marketing orientated firm recognises that the first step in applying a marketing system, which accepts the marketing concept as a major driving and co-ordinating force, is to become consumer orientated and examine the market. It will proceed to:

(a) assess consumer needs, wants and desires
(b) adapt and change the products to meet consumers: expectations
(c) persuade and influence customers to use a particular product or service
(d) evaluate the results of the product used and consumed

It follows therefore that some benefit can be gained by attempting to:

Understand and determine what influences consumer motivation and behaviour.

A consumer is influenced by ecnomic, cultural, sociological and psychological factors, and the fact that a human being has a memory means he can relate past experiences which guide him to future actions. Individuals however are influenced to different degrees, and behave differently according to the situation they find themselves in and the company they are with. Consequently predicting buyer behaviour will always be a challenge.

As a guide we can use the stages a buyer goes through when deciding to buy a product, and relate it to what the marketer is attempting to find out:

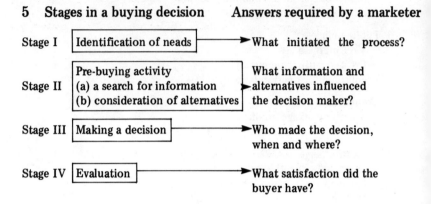

**5    Stages in a buying decision        Answers required by a marketer**

| | Stages in a buying decision | Answers required by a marketer |
|---|---|---|
| Stage I | Identification of neads | What initiated the process? |
| Stage II | Pre-buying activity<br>(a) a search for information<br>(b) consideration of alternatives | What information and alternatives influenced the decision maker? |
| Stage III | Making a decision | Who made the decision, when and where? |
| Stage IV | Evaluation | What satisfaction did the buyer have? |

In attempting to gather and evaluate the answers, they can provide a useful guide when:
- designing a product
- determining a price
- formulating a package
- building an image
- staging promotional activities

Let us now go through the stages of a buying decision:

### Stage I Identification of needs
Every person is motivated by internal basic needs, eg in order to survive we have to satisfy hunger and thirst. People are also goal-seekers and seek to purchase and consume to gratify acquired needs, or psychological needs, which have been developed and determined by sociological, cultural, economic and psychological factors.

Abraham Maslow, in his book *Motivation and Personality* (Harper and Row 1954) suggests that various needs are stronger than others at particular times, and that they can be set out in rank order, showing that as one need is satisfied an individual proceeds to another.

*Maslow: Hierarchy of needs*

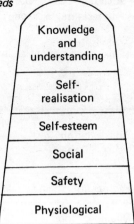

| | |
|---|---|
| (a)  Physiological | – the need to satisfy the bodily requirements |
| (b)  Security and safety | – the need to protect oneself |
| (c)  Social | – the need to belong, be recognised and accepted |
| (d)  Self-esteem | – the desire to satisfy one's 'ego' by possessing or doing things |
| (e)  Self-realisation | – the need to develop oneself to the maximum of one's capabilities |
| (f)  Knowledge and understanding | – these needs refer to the process of<br>– searching for a meaning in the things around us and the satisfaction of aesthetic needs. |

A marketing success of a hotel or catering unit often depends on the ability to satisfy several needs at the same time.

A meal can satisfy the physiological needs of hunger and survival, and eating it at home or within a known catering unit can provide security and safety. If we eat in the company of others it satisfies social needs, whilst self-esteem and self-realisation can be obtained by the environment, atmosphere, image, menu and price paid. The aesthetic pleasure comes from the presentation, texture, flavour and smell.

## Stage II    Pre-buying activity — how the choice is made
Consumers choose hotels and restaurants through:

(a)  past experience
(b)  opinions and impressions which present an image
(c)  comparative processes.

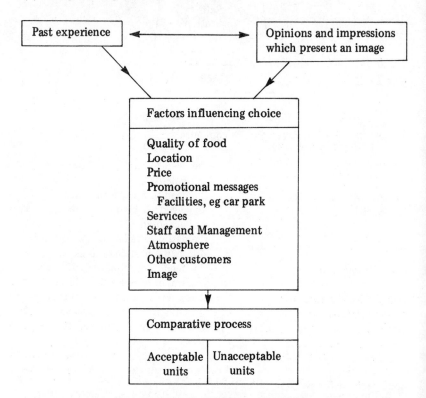

We can say that a consumer attempts to satisfy his requirement by selecting  an hotel or restaurant which has the correct image to suit the situation he finds himself in. He or she buys not one or two facts but several. In fact, he buys a package, which makes an image, consisting of the:

| | |
|---|---|
| **Product** | The services, facilities, atmosphere, differentiation and talking points |
| **Place** | The location and environment, driving more than 20 to 30 miles is usually unacceptable |
| **People** | The other customers they are likely to meet. Research tells us that 70% of people going for a drink went mainly to socialise |
| | The behaviour of management and staff and how to treat guests |

| | |
|---|---|
| Promotion | Publicity and sales can influence the image that is created |
| Price | This relates what is offered and what is acceptable to the customer. |

It is therefore very important that the package is presented so that each part fits together, integrating and guiding all departments and levels of management to selected market segments. This also means that we should consider too the ever-increasing rate of change within our society and be ready to act quickly.

## Stage III    Making the decision to buy

The actual choice will be influenced by two man factors:

1  a persons background, his age, education, life style, occupation, marital situation
2  the situation in which he finds himself, and:
    (i)   the time available
    (ii)  whether on business or on holiday
    (iii) the occasion, special or routine
    (iv)  the need— for diversion
                     — for self-gratification
                     — to satisfy hunger
                     — to impress others
                     — to socialise

## Stage IV    Evaluation

The experience gained from going to a restaurant or hotel is highly important not only in influencing your customer to come again but in obtaining word-of-mouth advertising.

David T Kollat, *Consumer Behaviour*, the Dryden Press, states that:

'visitors to a new food store, when asked what information was most unfluential in their decision to try the new store, indicated word-of-mouth twice as often as advertising and over three times more often than visual notice'

Many successful restaurants and hotels have similar statistics to show the effectiveness of a satisfied customer, and how they influence their friends.

### Summary

By attempting to understand buyer behaviour and in particular what motivates and influences him or her, we have identified some frameworks and patterns which will be helpful to analyse and understand situations before we plan for the future.

At least we can provide information to influence the decision maker and remind past customers by their previous experiences.

# Activities

## 1 Identifying factors that influence a person when choosing a restaurant

The factors influencing choice are numerous and changeable depending on the needs and wants at a particular time and perceived impressions. It is therefore difficult to state categorically which items are more important than others. Perhaps you could test this statement by carrying out the following activity:

Listed below are factors considered to be important when choosing a restaurant.

Licensed premises
Price
Quality and type of food
Speed of service
Cleanliness
Location
Atmosphere
Efficiency of management and staff
Promotional messages

Could you place these items in order of importance for:

(a) a person eating our regularly at lunch time, not on an expense account, and

(b) a person eating out, on a social occasion in the evening, eg once a month.

| | Lunch time | | Evening |
|---|---|---|---|
| (a) 1 | _____ | 1 | _____ |
| 2 | _____ | 2 | _____ |
| 3 | _____ | 3 | _____ |
| 4 | _____ | 4 | _____ |
| 5 | _____ | 5 | _____ |
| 6 | _____ | 6 | _____ |
| 7 | _____ | 7 | _____ |
| 8 | _____ | 8 | _____ |
| 9 | _____ | 9 | _____ |

You have no doubt identified different factors for the different situations. If you turn over the page, you will be able to compare the results of research carried out by Manchester Polytechnic students in 1978, which compared favourably with a survey carried out in London in 1964 by J C McKenzie, BSc Econ.

## 2   Self-assessment questions

After working through the study material and text books, test your knowledge by attempting to:

1   identify the most important environmental factors influencing the consumer.
2   describe how market segmentation can be used by a catering manager to increase consumer demand.
3   describe the factors influencing a buying decision.
4   identifiy the stages in a buying decision.

## 3   Test II

1   Describe how the 'marketing concept' affects the hotelier's approach to the operation of his business.
2   The number of holidays taken in Great Britain, by British people, has increased by only 50% over the last 20 years, compared with a doubling of overseas holidays every seven years.

| | Number of holidays by Britons in: | |
|---|---|---|
| | GB | Abroad |
| 1951 | 25 m | 1.5 m |
| 1972 | 37 m | 8.5m |

Describe the environmental factors which have influenced this trend.

3   The following statistics have been abstracted from the Annual Report on Household Food Consumption (Ministry of Agriculture, Fisheries and Food).

| | Grammes per week per person | | |
|---|---|---|---|
| | 1964 | 1974 | 1978 |
| Cheese | 90 | 105 | 106 |
| Butter | 170 | 159 | 129 |
| Potatoes | 1576 | 1296 | 1249 |
| Margarine | 96 | 99 | 101 |

State the possible reasons causing the changes in buyer behaviour.

Results of research by Manchester Polytechnic students covering several hundred respondents

| Lunch time | Evening |
|---|---|
| 1 Quality and type of food | 1 Quality and type of food |
| 2 Price | 2 Atmosphere |
| 3 Location | 3 Licensed premises |
| 4 Speed of service | 4 Price |
| 5 Atmosphere | 5 Efficiency of management and staff |
| 6 Cleanliness | 6 Promotional messages |
| 7 Efficiency of management & staff | 7 Location |
| 8 Licensed premises | 8 Speed of service |
| 9 Promotional messages | 9 Cleanliness |

**Note**
A survey by NOP Market Research found that 74% go to a pub with friends or to meet people. Perhaps it is a factor that is considered when 'eating out', eg do people gravitate towards a restaurant which will have customers with whom they wish to socialise.

**Summary**
In carrying out this activity, you will have become aware that the factors influencing the choice of a restaurant differ in importance according to need, situation and circumstances. Thus, showing the need to become consumer orientated and perhaps produce several packages for different markets from the same catering unit.

# III
# Marketing Reseach in the Hotel and Catering Industry

**Areas of study**
1 The scope of marketing research in the hotel and catering industry
2 Case studies
3 Case study I — Site selection
4 Feasibility studies in the hotel and catering industry
5 Case study II — A Feasibility study
6 Use of questionnaires

**Objectives**
On completing this chapter, the reader should be able to:
(a) explain and describe the nature of marketing research methods
(b) describe how marketing research can help in making decisions and operating a business
(c) explain how the hotelier and caterer can use marketing research

**Activities**
1 Questionnaire construction
2 Multiple choice questions on market research
3 Self-assessment questions
4 Test III

**Readings**
GILES, *Marketing*, Chapters V and VI
KOTAS, (editor) *Marketing orientation*, Chapters III and IV

## Marketing research in the hotel and catering industry

Marketing research has been defined as: 'the systematic collection, recording and analysis of data related to factors bearing on a business operation in an attempt to improve the efficiency and effectiveness of supply and demand'.

This definition highlights that marketing research is concerned with:
(a) collecting and recording information that can reduce the uncertainty of risk-taking and improve the quality of decisions, and
(b) all aspects of the business which relate to the exchange of products. In the case of the hotel and catering industry, this includes the analysis of markets, products, selling methods and financial and statistical results.

## 1 The scope of marketing research in the hotel and catering industry

Marketing research can be used to provide information for:

(a) problem solving
(b) planning, guiding and controlling current and future operations.

Within the industry information is usually analysed:

### 1 On markets
(a) To determine the location and size of demand in terms of quality and quantity, eg tourists, businessmen or local residents
(b) To ascertain the prospects of creating demand by area or social economic groups
(c) To ascertain the pattern of demand
(d) To determine the best market segments
(e) To determine consumer satisfaction rates.

### 2 On products
(a) The strengths and weaknesses of the company's products compared with competitors
(b) The trends of sales
(c) The satisfaction rates for various products.
(d) The activities of competitors relating to:
pricing
service
facilities
products
décor

### 3 On selling methods and results
(a) Sales campaigns
(b) Weak spots, departmental gross profits and occupancy rates
(c) Advertising effectiveness.

**Sources of information**
Information and data can be obtained in a variety of ways:

(a) *internal records* will provide information such as:
   — percentage occupancy rates
   — average spending power
   — sources of business
   — departmental profit margins.
(b) external sources — the local and national press; published local and national statistics, agencies, trade association, research organisations, professional bodies.
(c) *field research* can supply information on competitors' activities and what consumers' attitudes are towards certain products and services, this is normally collected by using:
   observation
   discussion groups
   questionnaires
   interviews — personal and telephone.

Note the case studies, later in the book, describe the statistics and their use in greater detail.

## The marketing research procedure
The usual procedure when carrying our research is to:

1  define the problem in writing, so all parties can agree with the objectives
2  determine the information and answers required
3  structure the procedure — the method of collecting information
4  design the sample, eg age, sex and social — economic groups
5  construct the questionnaire and make a pilot test
6  collect information
7  analyse data
8  prepare the report and recommendations.

## 2   Case studies

Throughout the remaining sections the author has introduced a series ot case studies which inter-relate and link the various factors within a marketing system.

The situations presented to the reader have been taken from consultancy and research projects, to give an insight into various techniques used in the hotel and catering industry.

The objectives behind the introduction of case studies are to give the reader practice in.

(a) identifying problems
(b) analysing information

(c)  making decisions

(d)  writing and presenting business-like reports

In general they also test knowledge and understanding and are a means of developing marketing and practical skills.

It should be remembered that there can be several solutions to the same problem, depending on how one interprets the information within the case, and how one sees it fitting into the marketing process.

## 3  Case study I — Site selection

**Objectives**

This case study has two main objectives:

1  to show how government statistics and field research, namely observation; can be used in the selection of a location for a catering unit

2  to let the student decide, from the figures provided the right site for the style of catering unit suggested by a company.

From the information provided, and the published statistics presented, select the town which you would recommend to Watson Ltd.

**Factors to be borne in mind when choosing a site for a catering unit**

A location analysis is made to provide information which will help to determine if a site or location will provide the right quality and quantity of business to:

1  provide a suitable return on capital invested

2  develop the company, whilst conforming to the marketing objectives.

**The catchment area**

This is the area from which customers can be expected to come.

Elements influencing a location —

(a)  numbers and types of customers living in the area

(b)  future development plans of the area

(c)  other business activities in the area

(d)  whether the area is a market town

(e)  tourist attractions

(f)  transport facilities.

**Several methods of assessment can be used**

1  Personal observation — examination of town and competitors.

2  Desk research —

    (a)  census of population, age, economic status of population

    (b)  census of distribution — retail sales for the area

    (c)  housing developments — from local authority.

**Summary**

1  The facts must be assessed with the marketing policy of the company

2  Expected profits must give a satisfactory return on capital.

**Watsons brief**

Watson Ltd of Cheshire have approached you to help them select a site for them to develop their business. The directors of the firm, in accordance with their expansion policy, wish to develop their restaurant business in a new area and at the same time invest money in a hotel which the son of the Chairman wishes to run. At present, Watsons have a well-established and successful outside catering business in Chester as well as their own bakery, delicatessen and grill type restaurant and snack bar presenting a variety of meals. The outside catering business — the main support of the company — operates at nearby race-courses, shows, weddings exhibitions, conferences and receptions.

Modifications have already been planned for the firm with the building of a blast freezing centre in Chester, which it is hoped will help in the development of their Cheshire business and that of the new site.

You are asked to investigate the potential for buying a hotel with a restaurant serving high class meals in the evening and a grill type fast food operation for lunches. Room for conferences, exhibitions and receptions would be desirable as they have established a reputation for this type of business.

The directors have stipulated that the new business should not be more than one hour's travelling distance by motor from Chester or the equivalent of approximately 40 miles, for ease of control of the operation. The cost of the hotel should not exceed £200,000.

The estate agents have provided you with five area which have hotels for sale suitable for the operation proposed:

|            |     |
|------------|-----|
| Ablethorpe | (A) |
| Bessington | (B) |
| Cransey    | (C) |
| Drankly    | (D) |
| Eppingford | (E) |

The company have described the hotel and catering unit it would like to operate, have emphasised that they attach a lot of importance to local residential trade to support the food side of the business through the restaurant, receptions and banquets.

You are asked to recommend the location within which they should open a new unit, after studying the information obtained by students of the local polytechnic from desk research and visits to the areas.

**Population trends:** (Census of population 1961 and 1971)

|   | 1961 | 1971 |
|---|------|------|
| A | 47,200 | 54,000 |
| B | 42,500 | 51,690 |
| C | 41,770 | 48,770 |
| D | 49,840 | 49,960 |
| E | 51,300 | 48,000 |

**Retail sales per head of population:** (Census of distribution 1970)

|   |   |
|---|---|
| A | £245 |
| B | £190 |
| C | £343 |
| D | £321 |
| E | £306 |

Note There is a correlation between where people shop and where they eat.

**Socio-economic group** — sample census 1966

|   | Professional employers manager | | Skilled manual | | Semi-skilled unskilled manual | |
|---|------|------|------|------|------|------|
|   | No. | % | No. | % | No. | % |
| E | 970 | 5.3 | 12,110 | 65.7 | 5,360 | 29.1 |
| C | 2,780 | 16.3 | 9,930 | 58.1 | 4,380 | 25.6 |
| D | 1,610 | 8.8 | 10,860 | 59.6 | 5,770 | 31.6 |
| B | 1,680 | 9.1 | 10,020 | 54.3 | 6,770 | 36.7 |
| A | 2,790 | 16.0 | 9,720 | 56.1 | 4,840 | 27.9 |

Note The first two groups are those with the highest income and consequently have the highest expenditure on eating out (as per Family Expenditure Survey MAFF).

**Car ownership** — Sample census 1966

% of households

|   | 1966 Population in households | With no car | With one car | With two car |
|---|------|------|------|------|
| C | 46,770 | 45.3 | 47.1 | 7.6 |
| A | 48,660 | 46.0 | 47.2 | 6.7 |
| B | 50,590 | 48.1 | 45.3 | 6.5 |
| E | 50,570 | 62.0 | 34.0 | 4.0 |
| D | 49,940 | 60.5 | 34.2 | 5.2 |

Estimated number of people likely to eat out in each area cenus of population 1971

From the total population of each area we have analysed the population categories who are not likely to eat out ie those with limited resources eg:

(a) population under 15
(b) population over 65
(c) the unemployed
(d) group E of the socio-economic groups

**Number of people**

|   | Under 15 | Over 65 | Unemployed | Group E |
|---|---|---|---|---|
| C | 11,460 | 6,250 | 1,896 | 4,380 |
| A | 12,620 | 5,850 | 1,683 | 4,840 |
| E | 11,670 | 6,610 | 1,976 | 5,360 |
| D | 12,000 | 5,610 | 1,280 | 5,770 |
| B | 13,460 | 5,970 | 2,709 | 6,770 |

**Personal observation**

A survey was carried out in the five areas as it was thought that the restaurants already open in the area would reflect the present requirements of the consumers.

Factors considered to be important when influencing consumers to choose a restaurant were itemised on a form and marks awarded out of 10 for each item when a restaurant was analysed.

The items considered were:

| | | |
|---|---|---|
| Type of service | Location | Decoration |
| Price | Size | Menu style |
| Identity | Related facilities | Quality |

The final summary showed the percentage of restaurants thought to be 'above average', average, and below average for each area.

| Area | No of restaurants Surveyed | Above average % | Average % | Below average % |
|---|---|---|---|---|
| C | 17 | 54 | 32 | 14 |
| D | 15 | 50 | 30 | 20 |
| E | 13 | 33 | 33 | 33 |
| A | 11 | 34 | 32 | 34 |
| B | 12 | 55 | 17 | 28 |

| TOWN | Population trends (A) | Retail sales per head (B) | Socio-economic Group (C) | Car ownership (D) | Number likely to eat out (E) | Observation (F) | TOTAL |
|---|---|---|---|---|---|---|---|
| | Points | Points | Points | Points | Points | Points | Points |
| A | | | | | | | |
| B | | | | | | | |
| C | | | | | | | |
| D | | | | | | | |
| E | | | | | | | |

TOWN recommended from the analysis — of desk research and observation

[              ]

**Note**  If you think certain factors are more important than others, add a weighting to them.

**Conclusion**

In actual fact the town selected by the students, though different to the one chosen by the directors, was accepted by the board as the right area for development.

# 4 Feasibility studies in the Hotel and Catering Industry

A feasibility study is an attempt to assess the market and its future potential, to determine whether a proposed unit should be built or developed to:

(a) provide a satisfactory return on capital invested, and
(b) fit into the present marketing policy of the owners.

## Procedure
To achieve the objectives a study is designed to provide a:

(a) market analysis
(b) competitors analysis
(c) product analysis, and
(d) financial analysis

*Diagram showing the factors influencing the decision to buy or build a catering unit*

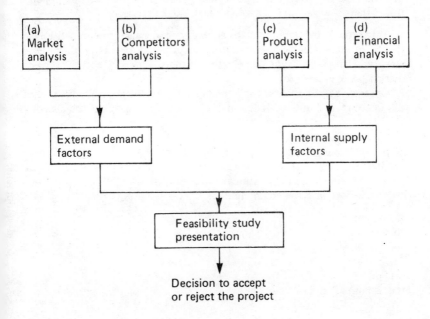

## (a) Market analysis
A market analysis attempts to identify the target market and customer wants and expectations. If the proposed unit is already operating then records will be available, if the venture is completely new then estimates and forecasts have to be made from observations and experience.

Consideration will be given to such factors as:

(i)   where the guests will come from — country, town, area
(ii)  what are the reasons for coming to the location — business, recreation, visiting family
(iii) how do the guests normally arrive — time and means of transport, rail, road or from airport
(iv)  the guests average spending power and length of stay
(v)   percentage of returning customers
(vi)  elements influencing the location — number and types of customers living in the area — future development plans for business and housing.

This type of information can help to pinpoint the primary and secondary markets and to determine if the expected demands can be supplied from the product that can be made available.

### (b) Competitors' analysis

Knowledge of the competitors in the area can be built up from guests, visits and observations, and provides information which can determine:

(i)   if all the market segments are being supplied
(ii)  the type of presentation, price, image, and facilities which are popular
(iii) if there is a 'gap' in the market which can be serviced.

This type of information helps an operator to assess the competition so that a product can be designed that is different or better than those already existing. The type of operators in the area also reflects the type of market being catered for.

Consequently the market and competitors analysis give an indication of the quantity and quality of the market needs which generate the demand.

### (c) Product analysis

A product analysis assesses the factors which make up the package or product offered by an hotel or restaurant. A comparison is usually made with competing units and consumer expectations.

The factors analysed could include:

(a)  location
(b)  image
(c)  facilities
(d)  services
(e)  prices
(f)  restaurant style

### (d) Financial analysis

A financial analysis provides details of the sales and profits of each department or sector, accommodation, food and beverage, and measures the estimated earnings in relation to the total investment made. The analysis will also show the capital expenditure and working capital requirements for the last financial year.

The product and financial analysis helps the operator determine whether the resources he has available can satisfy the market needs at a profit.

**Conclusion**
The feasibility study is then presented as a report usually with recommendations as to whether a proposed unit could be a financial success with the marketing policy of the organisation.

## 5  Case Study II — A Feasibility Study

This case provides practical data from an actual feasibility study. The objectives of presenting the case are to:

(a) enable the students to use quantitative and qualitative data to develop their ability to diagnose, evaluate and exercise abilities for sound and effective judgment
(b) present a relevant real-life situation to add to knowledge and understanding of marketing management and the hotel and catering industry.

### A marketing analysis before the opening of an hotel
The Chiltern Hotel had been suggested by the estate agents as a suitable establishment for development by Watson Ltd. Interviews with the surveyors and visits to the surrounding area have convinced the directors that the hotel was a good investment as far as the property and land was concerned, but, as they have had little experience of operating hotels, they asked us to carry out a feasibility study and to recommend whether or not they should purchase the hotel.

We agreed with the proposal and divided our investigation into four areas which, in total, helped us to make the right recommendation:

1  a current situation report
2  a product analysis
3  a market analysis
4  a financial analysis

### 1  A current situation report
The hotel had been in existence for 30 years, the present owners now wished to retire.

The image and reputation of the hotel seemed to be in doubt, but the location and the building itself looked good and no doubt new owners could achieve success.

The preliminary surveys showed that the management operated on a day-to-day basis and planning and control, marketing, preventive maintenance and budgetary control were simply not used. This became more apparent when a scrutiny of the financial accounts disclosed several disturbing features.

## 2  A product analysis

The resources of the hotel which were provided to satisfy customers: needs and wants, were analysed, assessed and, where possible, compared with competitors. The results are recorded below.

The hotel has a good restaurant and stands in two acres (0.80 hectares) of land which provides a spacious car park, gardens and room for expansion. It is situated in the centre of Cheshire, 15 miles from Manchester and 16 miles from Chester. There are frequent inter-city rail services from the local station, Hartford, which links to Crewe; London is approximately 2½ hours away by train. Three miles from the hotel is a motorway which links the main North/South M6 and East/West M63. The international airport, Ringway, brings over four million visitors each year and is situated six miles from the hotel. Swimming pools, golf courses and first class football and cricket clubs are within easy reach.

The hotel has 24 double bedrooms and planning permission for a further two double and ten single. The car park will take over 100 cars and the restaurant capacity is 100.

The exterior of the hotel is in reasonable condition, though since it was built 30 years ago the outside is in need of renovation. The bedrooms are well furnished, but without showers and toilets. It is estimated that for £5,000 showers and toilets could be placed in each room. The dining room, reception area and lounge create an excellent atmosphere by the colour and lighting schemes and high class furniture. Obviously the present owners took a pride in the restaurant.

**The Chiltern Hotel compared with the other two hotels in the area**

## 3  A market analysis

Within five miles of the hotel there are 140,000 people and within 15 miles 700,000, and the local planning authority anticipate a 10% increase during the next five years.

From the statistics available we were able to ascertain that:

1  approximately 75% of the guests came from the London area
2  the main reason for staying at the hotel was that business men did not like city centre hotels. Few people arrived from the motorway or airport
3  the restaurant and bar were used by the older members of the local population, and many business men tended to eat out at the airport hotel or local restaurant
4  local residents did not use the hotel for functions, nor did they recommend its use to friends
5  census of population showed the area contained a large proportion of 'A' and 'B' groups.

| | Chiltern | A railway hotel | An airport hotel |
|---|---|---|---|
| Site | In gardens | Centre of town | Concrete and gardens |
| Image (See test report) | Highly priced, old fashioned | Reasonably priced old fashioned | Modern |
| Facilities in bedrooms | No toilets/showers 24 doubles | Good — 50 doubles 50 singles | Good 200 singles |
| Rates charged — bed | £8 | £12 | £15 |
| Restaurant style | 100 — Silver Service ASP £4 | 200 — Silver Service ASP £6 | Fast food ASP £5 |
| Conference facilities | Excellent — limited by bedrooms | 100 — good (no car park) | None |
| Bar facilities | Free house — Good | Good | Good — Expensive |
| Facilties for functions | Good, but little used | Good (no car park) | None |

| Classification of working population | Within 5 miles | | Within 15 miles | |
|---|---|---|---|---|
| A — socio/economic group | 12,000 | 8.5 | 39,000 | 5.6 |
| B — " " " | 42,000 | 30.0 | 121,000 | 17.0 |
| Other groups | 86,000 | 61.5 | 540,000 | 77.4 |
| | 140,000 | 100.0 | 700,000 | 100.0 |

**Note** The average for Cheshire County A and B groups is 14.9%.

### Product awareness and image test

Three hundred people who usually eat out and live within 12 miles of the Chiltern Hotel were asked to:

Name *two* restaurants in the area they would go to or recommend

The results showed:

The Chiltern was only mentioned 20 times.

A second question was then asked:

Why have you not mentioned The Chiltern Hotel?

Results could be analysed into three headings

1 Too highly priced
2 Poor service
3 Did not know The Chiltern had a public restaurant.

The above results were disturbing but at least they showed alterations could be made to change the image and attract customers.

### Questions

To help the directors of Watson Ltd to decide whether or not to purchase The Chiltern Hotel

1 Describe the market segments best suited for the hotel.
2 What areas of the hotel should be adapted and changed to suit the market?
3 Write two paragraphs describing the advantages and benefits that could persuade potential customers to visit the hotel.

'A marketing manager is responsible for profitability', R M S Wilson, *Management Controls on Marketing*. It follows therefore that he should be able to interpret and use accounting figures to make decisions and plans for the future.

## 4    A financial analysis

The financial accounts for the year ending 31 October 1981 were very disappointing and alarming. But our objectives were to determine the true worth of the hotel for the future rather than look back at the past.

It was therefore necessary to analyse the accounts in detail to show the true potential and to show up the limitations of historic accounts and the benefits of management accounts which are used to help in the process of planning, co-ordinating, motivating and controlling the activities of an organisation.

This section shows:

(a)  the accounts as they were originally presented
(b)  how they were redesigned to give more information.


## FINANCIAL ACCOUNTS — CHILTERN HOTEL

## PROFIT AND LOSS ACCOUNT — YEAR ENDING 31 OCTOBER 1981

|  | 1981 £ | 1980 £ |
|---|---|---|
| **Income** | | |
| Charges to customers | 114,650 | 100,500 |
| **Expenditure** | | |
| Purchases of provisions | 33,400 | 33,150 |
| Wages | 40,200 | 34,450 |
| Establishment expenses | 26,450 | 25,800 |
| Administration expenses | 15,650 | 12,850 |
| Financial expenses | 5,500 | 4,900 |
| TOTAL EXPENDITURE | 121,200 | 111,150 |
| Net Trading LOSS | 6,500 | 10,650 |

**BALANCE SHEET** as at 31 October, 1981

|  |  | 1981 |  | 1980 |
|---|---|---|---|---|
|  |  | £ |  | £ |
| Fixed assets (net) |  | 141,600 |  | 142,000 |
| Current assets | 9,350 |  | 11,000 |  |
| Less: |  |  |  |  |
| Current liabilites | 17,450 | - 8,100 | 13,000 | - 2,000 |
| NET ASSETS |  | 133,500 |  | 140,000 |
|  |  |  |  |  |
| Financed by: |  |  |  |  |
| Share capital/reserves |  | 111,450 |  | 118,000 |
| Loans |  | 22,050 |  | 22,000 |
|  |  | 133,500 |  | 140,000 |

Note
The size of the loss, current liabilities and loan were rather disturbing

To determine the true situation, it was decided to analyse the accounts in two stages:

1    to produce departmental accounts, by analysing 530 invoices and allocating expenses to each section, and
2    to deduct items which would not occur if the hotel was purchased by new owners.

## Stage I Departmental accounts

The departmental accounts showed the gross and net profit ratios, which when compared with other units of a similar size showed up interesting results.

| | Rooms £ | % | Food £ | % | Beverage £ | % | Total £ | % |
|---|---|---|---|---|---|---|---|---|
| Sales | 53,200 | 100 | 38,700 | 100 | 22,750 | 100 | 114,650 | 100 |
| Less: Cost of goods sold | | | 17,400 | 45 | 16,000 | 70 | 33,400 | 29 |
| GROSS PROFIT | 53,200 | 100 | 21,300 | 55 | 6,750 | 30 | 81,250 | 71 |
| Less: Wages/staff costs | 17,100 | 32 | 16,400 | 42 | 3,500 | 15 | 37,000 | 31 |
| Net margin | 36,100 | 68 | 4,900 | 13 | 3,250 | 15 | 44,250 | 40 |
| Less: Allocated expenses | 13,082 | 24 | 4,551 | 12 | 1,483 | 7 | 19,116 | 18 |
| Departmental operating profit | 23,018 | 44 | 349 | 1 | 1,767 | 8 | 25,134 | 22 |
| Less: Other expenses | | | | | | | 31,684 | 28 |
| Hotel operating LOSS | | | | | | | 6,550 | -6 |

---

**Activity**

The Inter-Hotel Comparison Data, published to Strathclyde University showed:

**The median efficiency of 50 bedroom hotels**

|  | Sales | Direct materials | Wages | Net margin |
|---|---|---|---|---|
| Accommodation | 100 | – | 18 | 82 |
| Food | 100 | 43 | 42 | 15 |
| Beverage | 100 | 46 | 23 | 31 |

By comparing the ratios of the hotel with the Strathclyde figures, state two areas which need attention, consider the possible reasons for the difference.

---

After making ratio analysis comparisons it was discovered that:

(a) the wage of a maid, working in the owner's house, was included in the accommodation wage accounts. This had been overlooked by the auditors and was illegal . . . . . . £1,500
(b) the cost of drinks appeared to be high, but this was caused by pilfering, cash and stock to the value of approximately . . . . . .£5,000

**Stage II  Identifying non-recurring items in the accounts**

1   The financial expenses of bank interest and bank charges would not occur if a new company took over . . . . . . £2,750
2   Capital items that had been incorrectly charged to revenue, £7,000 for fire precautions and insurance payments on owner's life £1,462 would not be incurred in the future . . . . . . £8,462

**Note**
The true state of affairs after taking into account the items above, suggests that a profit of £11,262 could be expected, rather than a loss of £6,550.

---

Calculate the return on capital as a percentage
if the profit of £11,262 was obtained

---

**The result of the feasibility study**
After considering the financial, product and marketing aspects, and observing the large amount of business the competitors were doing, we advised the purchase of the hotel.

We thought that:

(a) the accommodation, now with a 50% occupancy rate could be increased to over 60%, and the restaurant business considerably improved, particularly at lunch-time
(b) the property with the land would be a good investment for the future as the land and buildings would follow the inflationary trend, more so than money in the bank
(c) the hotel's restaurant would act as an outlet for some of the products the company produces
(d) it provided a suitable managerial post for the chairman's son.

We estimated that profit after tax could be £19,000 approximately.

Taking into account all the above factors, plus the fact that the present owner wished to sell quickly because of the bank calling in the outstanding loan, we considered £140,000 for the premises and fixtures a reasonable price. The owner also accepted £9,000 for stock and debtors, valued at £3,700 and £5,500 respectively.

The offer was accepted and the sale was completed on 31 December, 1977.

**Question**
1   Draw up a Balance Sheet for the 1 January 1981. Watson Ltd, the new owners paid cash.
2   Show, as a percentage, the return on capital expected, after tax.

3   State the two areas of concern shown in the statistics below, related to The Chiltern Restaurant, and describe the steps you would take to correct the situation.

Investigation of restaurant and kitchen trading results Nov 1980 to Oct 81

### Food costs as percentage of sales

| Quarter 1980/81 | Food cost £ | Sales £ | Food cost x 100 Sales |
|---|---|---|---|
| Nov to Jan | 4,190 | 9,910 | 42.3% |
| Feb to April | 4,230 | 10,060 | 42.0% |
| May to July | 4,410 | 9,840 | 44.8% |
| Aug to Sept | 4,570 | 8,890 | 51.4% |
| | 17,400 | 38.700 | 45.0% |

## 6 The use of questionnaires

While methods of research are improving all the time, particularly methods related to motivational research and in-depth interviewing, basic methods, such as the use of questionnaires, can still be operated by unit managers, which will yield information to guide operations.

The next few pages present:

(a) guidelines in constructing a questionnaire
(b) questionnaires presently being used within the industry
(c) an activity, helping the reader to identify the difficulties in constructing questionnaires.

## 1 Questionnaire construction

A questionnaire is a highly important aspect of marketing research and students should study and familiarise themselves with the construction and format that are presented in various books on the subject. The notes below are intended as guidelines only.

### Form of questionnaire

The questionnaire is usually divided into four parts:

1 *the classification of respondents* — this requires such details of the respondent as sex, age, marital status, occupation
2 *the identification of the survey and interviewer* — this is for filing purposes and to cross check the work of the interviewer
3 *the provision of a control question* — to check one answer against another to check on the reliability of the respondent
4 *the questions related to the subject-matter of the enquiry* .

### Important guidelines to consider when constructing a questionnaire

1 Definition of problem and purpose of the survey
2 The use of a pilot survey, to alter and improve the original
3 Questions should be easily understood and not ambiguous
4 Questions should be designed to have a precise answer
5 Questions should not rely too much on memory
6 Questions should not be biased
7 Questions should not require calculations to be made
8 Questions should be presented in a logical sequence
9 Personal questions should be left until the end
10 Information should be collected in boxes to help analysis
11 Design and layout should help the respondent and researcher so that information can be collected, recorded and filed easily
12 Words of gratitude to the respondent should be expressed.

The student is now asked to study the questionnaires on the next two pages, which have been used in the industry, and any other questionnaire he can obtain and then carry out the activity which has been designed to test his knowledge and understanding.

We should very much appreciate your comments about the various departments, members of staff and amenities listed by ticking the appropriate boxes:

1. RECEPTION   Good   Fair   Poor      Good   Fair   Poor

    The Porter   ☐ ☐ ☐   The Receptionist   ☐ ☐ ☐

    The Cashier   ☐ ☐ ☐

2. BEDROOM

    Decoration   ☐ ☐ ☐   Lighting   ☐ ☐ ☐

    Beds   ☐ ☐ ☐   Cleanliness   ☐ ☐ ☐

    Furniture   ☐ ☐

3. BATHROOMS      ☐ ☐ ☐

4. THE NIGHT PORTERS      ☐ ☐ ☐

5. THE BAR STAFF      ☐ ☐ ☐

6. TELEPHONE SERVICE      ☐ ☐ ☐

7. RESTAURANT SERVICE      ☐ ☐ ☐

8. Why did you choose this hotel

    By chance ☐     Have stayed previously ☐

    Company booking ☐     On personal recommendation ☐

    Credit Card ☐     Travel Agent Booking ☐

              Booked by a Centre Hotel

9. Did you find it convenient for ☐

    Business ☐     Sightseeing ☐

    Shops ☐     Entertainment ☐

10. If you used the hotel's conference and banqueting facilities what was your opinion:

. . . . . . . . . . . . . . . . . . . . . . . . . . . . . . . . . . . . . . . . . . . . . . . . . . . . .

. . . . . . . . . . . . . . . . . . . . . . . . . . . . . . . . . . . . . . . . . . . . . . . . . . . . .

. . . . . . . . . . . . . . . . . . . . . . . . . . . . . . . . . . . . . . . . . *Continued*

11. For what did you like this hotel best:

. . . . . . . . . . . . . . . . . . . . . . . . . . . . . . . . . . . . . . . . . . . . . . . .

. . . . . . . . . . . . . . . . . . . . . . . . . . . . . . . . . . . . . . . . . . . . . . . .

12. What should be improved immediately (or any other comments you may have time to make):

. . . . . . . . . . . . . . . . . . . . . . . . . . . . . . . . . . . . . . . . . . . . . . . .

. . . . . . . . . . . . . . . . . . . . . . . . . . . . . . . . . . . . . . . . . . . . . . . .

. . . . . . . . . . . . . . . . . . . . . . . . . . . . . . . . . . . . . . . . . . . . . . . .

. . . . . . . . . . . . . . . . . . . . . . . . . . . . . . . . . . . . . . . . . . . . . . . .

. . . . . . . . . . . . . . . . . . . . . . . . . . . . . . . . . . . . . . . . . . . . . . . .

. . . . . . . . . . . . . . . . . . . . . . . . . . . . . . . . . . . . . . . . . . . . . . . .

HOTEL . . . . . . . . . . . . . . . . . . . .ARRIVAL DATE . . . . . . . . . . . .

NAME. . . . . . . . . . . . . . . . . .ROOM NO. . . . . . . . . . . . . . . . .

Please post this form, which is already addressed and for which the postage is pre-paid.

Thank you very much indeed for the trouble you have taken.

Please do not hesitate to ask for the Duty Manager and speak to him if you have any comments to make concerning the amenities and services provided while you are staying at the hotel.

**A PATIENT OPINION SURVEY**

| | | VERY POOR | POOR | ABOUT RIGHT | GOOD | VERY GOOD |
|---|---|---|---|---|---|---|
| TASTE | BREAKFAST | | | | | |
| | LUNCH | | | | | |
| | SUPPER | | | | | |

| | | | | | | |
|---|---|---|---|---|---|---|
| APPEARANCE | BREAKFAST | | | | | |
| | LUNCH | | | | | |
| | SUPPER | | | | | |
| | | | | | | |

| | | | | | | |
|---|---|---|---|---|---|---|
| CHOICE & VARIETY | BREAKFAST | | | | | |
| | LUNCH | | | | | |
| | SUPPER | | | | | |
| | | | | | | |

| | | FAR TOO SMALL | TOO SMALL | ABOUT RIGHT | TOO BIG | FAR TOO BIG |
|---|---|---|---|---|---|---|
| QUANTITY | BREAKFAST | | | | | |
| | LUNCH | | | | | |
| | SUPPER | | | | | |

| | | TOO COLD | ABOUT RIGHT | TOO HOT |
|---|---|---|---|---|
| TEMPERATURE | BREAKFAST | | | |
| | LUNCH | | | |
| | SUPPER | | | |

PATIENTS COMMENTS:

53

# Activities

## 1   Questionnaire construction

A catering manager will often require information which involves an attempt to measure attitudes, opinions, behaviour and responses. It is usual to collect and record this information on a questionnaire, because

(a)  the questions are in a systematic order
(b)  the answers can be recorded systematically.

To develop an awareness of the difficulties of constructing a questionnaire could you carry out the following activity, taking care to suggest alternatives if you think a statement or question is incorrect.

### Activity

A tour operator wishes to indentify the factors influencing the choice of hotel-based package holidays. He has produced a questionnaire and wishes you to read it through and point out and later anything which needs to be changed or has been missed.

**Questionnaire**

**Objective** To identify factors influencing the choice of hotel-based package holidays.

Name Mr/Mrs/Miss

Address

Age

Marital status

Occupation

**Please tick the relevant box**

1  Have you ever taken a package holiday outside the UK    Yes  ☐
   No  ☐

   *If 'No' close interview*

2  Which of the following lengths of package holiday    7 days  ☐
   would you be most likely to take    10 days  ☐
   14 days  ☐

3  How much money would you be prepared to pay    ☐

4  Would you not agree that package holidays abroad    No  ☐
   are not more expensive than holidays in the UK    Yes  ☐

5  More and more people are taking self-catering    No  ☐
   holidays. Have you ever considered them?    Yes  ☐

6  Which activities are *important* to you when considering the choice of a summer package holiday?

   | 1 |
   | 2 |
   | 3 |
   | 4 |
   | 5 |
   | 6 |

7  What paper do you read?

   | 1 | 2 |

Thank you for your co-operation

Outline answer

**Letter to tour operator**
The main problems in constructing a questionnaire lie in its:

(a)  construction and framework
(b)  identifying what should be asked
(c)  the wording of the question.

Under these three headings I would like to make the following suggestions.

**A  Construction and framework**
1  'introduction' should be included, which explains in more detail for what and why you are wanting the information. It usually leads to more co-operation from the respondents.
2  To test co-operation many questionnaires will include a control question which checks on the response of a previous question and one of these should be included.
3  The answer box to question 7, should be placed to the right hand side of the paper, to aid analysis and recording.

**B  Identifying what should be asked**
In identifying the respondent there could be problems in:

(a)  asking for their age, could you include an age range scale
(b)  marital status, the wording should be altered as it is not always understood.

**C  The wording of the questions**
1  Question 3 is rather vague. Could you reword to include the words 'per adult' and clarify that the time period is the same as in question 2
2  Question 4 contains a double negative and makes it impossible to answer
3  Question 5 is a leading question and unacceptable
4  Question 6 relies on memory; whilst it is good to have an open-ended question, could some guidelines be given, eg
    — influence of family and friends
    — cost
    — period of year
    — promotion
    -- destination
    — hotel
    — company
5  Question 7 could lead to complications; there is a difference between reading a newspaper and buying a newspaper on a regular basis.

## 2 Multiple choice questions on market research

From the following statements choose what you consider to be the correct answer:

1 Marketing research seeks mainly to:
(a) improve the efficiency and effectiveness of supply and demand
(b) measure the spending power of segments of the market
(c) solve problems
(d) analyse results.

2 A market analysis is mainly concerned with:
(a) prices charged by competitors
(b) identifying market trends
(c) selecting market segments suitable for the unit
(d) analysing current needs and wants.

3 A product analysis is mainly concerned with:
(a) the food and beverage offered by competitors
(b) all the factors which make up the package offered by a catering unit
(c) identifying the main selling points of a product or unit
(d) measuring consumer opinions about the products offered.

4 The main method used to obtain consumer satisfaction rates for an hotel is by using:
(a) observation
(b) secondary data
(c) a survey
(d) a questionnaire.

## 3 Self-assessment questions

After working through the study material and text books test your knowledge by answering the following questions:

1 What are the functions of marketing research?
2 What is a market analysis?
3 What is a product analysis?
4 What is a feasibility study?
5 Why is a questionnaire important for recording the results of a personal interview?

## 4  Test paper III

1 Describe and evaluate the various phases in carrying out a feasibility study for a hotel.
2 What is the difference between 'marketing research' and 'market research'? Describe briefly the main methods used when carrying out a market research survey.
3 How is it possible to segment the market for guests?
4 Indicate the main factors to be borne in mind prior to research investigations. Describe the main kinds of data and show how they may be applied to areas of the hotel and catering industry.

# IV
# Marketing Planning

**Areas of study**
1 The marketing plan
2 The marketing mix
3 Product planning
4 Product planning and the use of the product life cycle

**Objectives**
On completing this chapter the reader should be able to:
(a) describe the framework of a marketing plan
(b) discuss the significance of the product life cycle
(c) describe the main components in a marketing mix

**Activities**
1 Self-assessment questions
2 Test IV

**Readings**
GILES, *Marketing*, Chapter IV
KOTAS, *Marketing Orientation*, Chapter IV, V, VI, VII

All hotel and catering organisations should produce a marketing plan for the group and each unit. The plan will determine the course of the business towards the most suitable markets and the most effective way of organising resources.

Planning provides:

1 A framework of objectives, policies and strategies to guide decision-making which prevents 'management by crisis' and the use of ad hoc decisions
2 A powerful channel of communications for people within the company with the means to measure and evaluate progress.

## 1   The marketing plan

From the product, market and financial analysis a marketing plan is developed to meet certain objectives which are related to meeting market needs at a profit. All factors which can be controlled by management are considered in the plan. Some marketing experts classify these factors as product, place, promotion, price and profitability. A further consideration is the uncontrollable factors in the environment, particularly competition.

A statement in writing is usually produced in realistic terms and communicated to the members of staff concerned with operational management in the following form.

**1   An historical revue and current situation report covering:**
(a)  the products and services
(b)  the market
(c)  the financial aspects
(d)  the competition

**2   Statement of marketing objectives**
This is expressed in several ways usually quantified and related to a time period, usually one year, it normally contains a *profit plan* analysed to show:

(i)   the return on capital invested
(ii)  sales turnover — occupancy percentages, food covers
(iii) departmental gross profit margins.

**3   A plan of action through**
(a)  the *product* — this will include recipes, portion sizes, garniture and presentation. The concept also includes the beverage, dining and accommodation environment services and facilities
(b)  the *price* — the determination of selling prices and promotional discounts

(c) the *place* -- the selection and maintenance of sites, a study of location, and the creation of atmosphere

(d) *promotion* - including advertising, sales techniques, creaton of the image, merchandising and the establishment of promotional or package prices.

**4  Methods of evaluation and control**

(a) the establishment of standards, the comparison of actual results with a standard on a weekly or four weekly basis

(b) the way corrective action is taken

A marketing plan provides a clear statement of each objective and careful consideration of methods, policies, procedures and time which will apply to each objective.

## Advantages of marketing planning

1  It determines priorities

2  It leads to effective integration, as agreement has to be reached on the most effective use of reserves to reach the objectives

3  Planning also precedes a measure of expected performance during a particular time period.

## Rolling plans

Though a marketing plan is usually made yearly, as it fits naturally into a financial year, many catering organisations plan over a period of five years or even longer. Therefore, at the end of the year, progress is reviewed and evaluated towards meeting the long term objectives.

The advantages are.

(a) a firm can be guided towards a long-term target rather than make many changes of direction

(b) it allows for the development of certain sections or departments in order of priority rather than developing everything at once.

## 2   The marketing mix

The marketing plan will describe how management is trying to combine or mix several variables to satisfy specified consumer needs highlighted by market segmentation. In the hotel and catering industry a marketing manager is concerned with four factors, classified as the four Ps:

Product
Place and channels of distribution
Promotion
Price

They represent the variables a manager can control and which determine the nature of the package offered to potential customers to produce a fifth P — profitability.

A list of the particular variables within each P is provided in the table below.

*Elaboration of the 'four P's'*

| Product | Place/Channels | Promotion | Price |
|---|---|---|---|
| Quality | Distribution channels | Advertising | Level |
| Features and Options | | | |
| Style | Distribution coverage | | Discounts |
| Brand name | | Personal selling | Allowances |
| Packaging | Outlet locations | | |
| Service level | | Sales promotion | Payment terms |
| Other services | Transportation | Publicity | |

Source, KOTLER, P., *Marketing Management,* Prentice Hall 1976

These items will be evaluated separately, but it should be bourne in mind that the four Ps are inter-related and that they are influenced by:
(i)   past performances
(ii)  existing resources
(iii) the current marketing environment
(iv)  company policy.

Note The application of the marketing mix is made within the case studies described in Chapter VI — Pricing.

## 3   Product planning

Product planning involves those planning activities which attempt to marry-up the product to the market expectations. Market research describes the needs, wants and desires and product planning converts the knowledge into saleable packages. Product planning is a continuous process constantly reacting to changes caused by uncontrollable factors, such as:

— competition
— changes in food consumption habits
— economic conditions and employment levels
— technological factors
— political and government influences
— population changes.

Product planning is an essential component of the marketing mix, directed at identified market segments.

## What is the product

A customer buys benefits and experiences rather than products. For example, a restaurant does not just offer meals, but flavour, portion sizes, garniture and colour. In fact we could extend the meal, to include atmosphere, image, facilities and service found in the premises. Consequently we must see the 'product' as a package consisting of:

1 *the quality and standard* of accommodation, food and drink provided
2 *the image* — ie, appearance and atmosphere of the premises
3 *the service* — the interpersonal relationship, the speed of operation, the numbers of hours available
4 *the facilities* — bars, restaurants, swimming pool, television lounges.

These four items are usually considered separately when reviewing the present situation and allocating money for development and change.

## The Scope of product planning

The main factors in product planning are as follows:

(a) identifying changes in the current situation, eg buying habits
(b) analysing competitors' activities
(c) determining adjustments and developments that have to be made and the order of priority for the allocation of funds

*Diagram showing the product planning function*

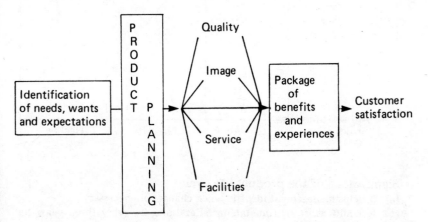

## 4 Product planning and the use of the product life cycle

The three main functional areas of a hotel: accommodation, food and beverage can each have different patterns of sales over a period of years. Some firms can identify the trends and use them in product planning, by relating them to the concept of the product life cycle.

The concept of the product life cycle presents a view that every product has a life span and that from the date of introduction it is heading for its demise. Naturally alterations have to be made to a product, particularly a hotel which is built to last 50 years or more, if the demise is to be averted. What product planning will ensure, is that alterations are made after identifying current and future needs and wants of the customers.

In the hotel and catering industry product differentiation is often used when designing new products, so we should perhaps use the relationship between having a different or distinctive type of product, and the life cycle and the need for change. (see diagram)

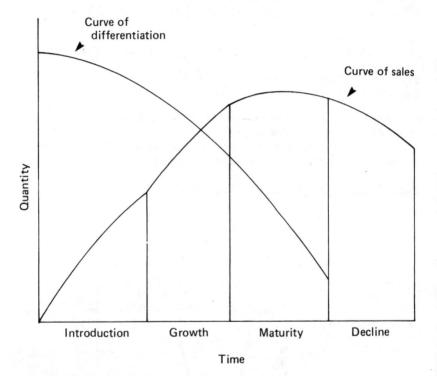

## Significance of the product life cycle
(a) It helps management identify when changes are necessary
(b) It could assist in time-tabling alterations, eg every three years the restaurant should be redesigned
(c) Priorities can be allocated to different products, according to sales patterns and the period of differentiation
(d) It highlights the areas for research and development.

The product life cycle, and its use with product planning, directs management to the market place to assess change and competition before making costly and expensive alterations.

**Plans for the 'Place' and channels of distribution**

A major element of the marketing mix is the place or location and channels of distribution.

Place or location refers to the location of a unit and the way product, services and information are made available to consumers. Location, often the key to success is fixed once the investment is made and therefore we will concentrate our attention on the channels of distribution.

All hoteliers are seeking to make themselves known to potential customers who are spread over a large geographical area and have many varied incomes, interests and needs, but few units can afford the promotional costs.

**Direct channels**   The simplest channel of distribution is when the hotelier chooses to sell his goods direct to the consumer, using a salesman, usually himself or impersonal methods such as direct-mail.

**Indirect channels**   The consumer need for more information, lower prices, and complete packages has produced an increase in the number of organisations which look after travel and hotel arrangements. They include:

| | |
|---|---|
| Tour operators | All these organisations are concerned with making |
| Travel agents | arrangements for people needing hospitality, and |
| Chambers of commerce | will use or promote hotels to satisfy consumer needs |
| Airlines | and wants. |

Hotels can benefit from the promotional efforts of intermediaries and thought has to be given as to whether the advantages outweigh the costs.

# Activities

## 1    Self-assessment questions

After working through the study material and text books, test your knowledge by:

1   Outlining and describing the basic features which a marketing plan should include.
2   Defining planning.
3   Stating the stages of the product life cycle?
4   Describing 'product planning' and relate it to the hotel and catering industry.
5   Defining the four Ps?

## 2    Test IV

1   How does the concept of the product life cycle help in operating a hotel or restaurant.
2   Discuss the importance of the marketing mix to management in the hotel and catering industry.
3   Prepare a marketing plan for a hotel of 50 bedrooms. Describe the information you would include and how you would ensure that the plan is operating effectively.

# V
# Promotion

**Areas of study**
1  Planning a promotion programme
2  Promotion media used in the industry
(i)    personal selling
(ii)   advertising
(iii)  direct mail
(iv)   sales promotion
(v)    merchandising
(vi)   public relations
(vii)  agents
3  Re-opening the Chiltern Hotel. A case study

**Objectives**
On completing this chapter the reader should be able to:
(a)  describe the role of promotion
(b)  describe the factors considered in a promotion campaign
(c)  discuss the advantages of using an advertising agency
(d)  compare the relative merits of the variety of the media used

**Activities**
1  Formulating promotion plans
2  An in-depth study of advertising
3  Self-assessment questions
4  Test V

**Readings**
GILES, *Marketing*, Chapters VI and VII
KOTAS, *Marketing Orientation*, Chapters VIII and IX

*Promotion*

**The meaning of promotion**

Having ascertained the potential consumer's needs and wants through marketing research, and planned our product accordingly, we are now ready to activate the process, which brings the buyer and seller together, through PROMOTION.

Promotion is the process by which consumers are:

(a) made aware of a catering unit
(b) persuaded to visit the unit
(c) encouraged to return to the unit.

Perhaps this can be best illustrated in diagrammatic form:

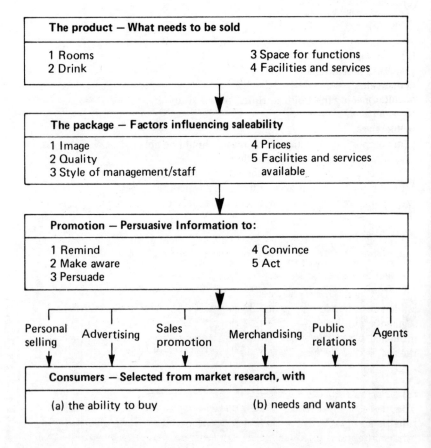

*The above diagram shows how 'Promotion' fits into the marketing system*

# 1  Planning a promotion programme

Promotion is an activity which needs to be carefully planned, co-ordinated and controlled. The normal practice in the hotel and catering industry is to consider a promotional plan each year, worked out in the form of a campaign.

The process will include:

(a)  determing objectives
(b)  defining the market segments
(c)  formulating the messages
(d)  timing of promotion
(e)  budgeting
(f)  selecting the media
(g)  evaluation of results

### (a)  Determing objectives

Usually the main objective of a promotion campaign is to stimulate demand by communicating persuasive messages. The management has to decide the particular emphasis that has to be projected at a particular time to a particular market segment, for example, the campaign messages can be used to:

(i)  *inform* prospective buyers what is available in the form of facilities available, times of opening, prices, etc.
(ii)  *remind* past users of the continuing existence of the establishment
(iii)  *persuade* new customers to use the establishment in the future
(iv)  *convince* prospective customers that the product is good and will be beneficial to the user
(v)  *establish* in the prospective customers' mind the *differential values* of your product compared with competitors.

### (b)  Defing the market segments

Market research findings will have established the best markets and market segments, and have guidelines for the right kind of messages to project to influence buyer behaviour. It can also determine the best media to reach the age, sex, social class, income level, location, etc, desired.

### (c)  Formulating the messages

The messages must relate to the objective decided upon, and at the same time be acceptable to the market segment aimed at. They must therefore attract attention, generate interest and inform. Basically our product has been designed to satisfy a consumer need, so we should formulate the message in a way which shows a benefit will pass to the consumer if the product is consumed.

69

Note Designing a message and selecting media is beyond the scope of the book, it is only intended to outline some of the problems that are presented. Help in solving these problems should perhaps be sought by consulting the specialists — advertising agents. Their work is briefly described later in this chapter.

### (d) Timing of promotion

The time promotion takes place will depend on the objectives, and *when the decision is made to purchase.*

(i) summer holidays are decided upon mainly during December, January and Feburary, and it is usual for 75% of the promotion budget to be spent during this period

(ii) A decision to make a week-end visit to a restaurant is often made during the week, hence the media used is often a local weekly paper

(iii) Consumers of meals at lunch-time may be attracted at the point of sale, and promotion, will be immediate and daily through signs and displays at the unit.

### (e) Budgeting

The cost of promotion is usually related to the objectives, sales turnover of the operation and the benefits one hopes to achieve.

It is always difficult to determine how much should be spent, and we may have to be guided by the specialist. In the industry several methods are used, such as:

(i) a fixed percentage of current or estimated sales, for example many operations use 2% of turnover as a guide in the UK. In the USA the figure is nearer 3%. The weakness of this system, is that as sales fall, so does promotion expenditure, when perhaps promotional activities should increase when sales fall

(ii) matching to the main competitor. This system is difficult to apply, as details are sometimes difficult to obtain and competitors have different objectives and often different markets

(iii) a cost per unit sold, or in the case of hotels, money allocated on the basis of rooms not being sold

(iv) what the operation can afford, this method is still widely used, but has little to recommend it, as it relates to production orientated operations

(v) determining what has to be spent to meet the objectives laid down by management

Many organisations now consider that rather than use methods related to what others do, or with what happened last year, method (v) should be used as it is related to specific objectives.

**(f) Selecting the media**

The choice of media will depend on how one wishes the messages to be transferred from producer to customer, and the relative cost per 1,000 potential customers.

*Advertising* has been defined as paid for messages, describing the business in a favourable way, using posters, newspapers, television, radio, direct mail, magazines.

*Personal selling* is a personal approach to a prospective customer which has the advantage of a salesman being on the spot to answer objections, meet problems and follow through to the completion of the sale.

*Sales promotion* has been described as those activities closely connected to the day to day operations and are usually controlled directly by the firm itself, for example:
   − trade discount offers
   − price reductions
   − special offers.

*Merchandising* includes all activities to increase sales, that take place within the unit, eg displays and sales by the dining room staff.

*Public relations* is concerned with building up the 'image' and 'standing' of the operation in the public's mind. It attempts to create a favourable attitude in the minds of present and future customers, employees, and investors, and therefore is not usually directly related to a particular product or service.

*Agents* Trade associations, travel agencies and tour operators will promote your operation in their literature for the benefit of their members.

**(g) Evaluation of results**

The effectiveness of promotion should be related to the marketing objectives. Unfortunately the methods used for measuring results have their limitations. But every attempt should be made to make some form of assessment.

The following methods are sometimes used:

(i)   enquiries received from a particular publication or activity
(ii)  analysing sales figures
(iii) measuring public awareness of a product before and after promotion
(iv)  actual sales in 'test markets'.

## Use of an advertising agency

Managers in the catering industry must know the fundamentals of promotional planning. But, as the work is spasmodic and requires specialised skill and experience, it is often necessary to seek help from agencies.

The service an agency provides include:

(a) assistance with marketing research in identifying the customer's needs and wants

71

(b) help with determing marketing objectives and the operational plans to reach the objectives
(c) the provision of creative talent to design 'copy' and layout
(d) assistance in selecting media and working out a plan of approach
(e) assistance in carrying out a public relations programme
(f) methods of evaluating the effectiveness of an advertising campaign.

Any operation is likely to use the resources allocated to promotion more effectively by using an advertising agency. The staff and expertise of the agency are available at any time for advice about the fundamentals of marketing and promotion, without being on the full-time staff.

## 2 Promotional media used in the industry

### (i) Personal selling

Personal selling is a personal approach to the prospective customer which has the advantage of a salesman being on the spot to answer objections, meet problems and follow through to the completion of the sale. A salesman can create product awareness, arouse interest, and negotiate terms and prices to the mutual benefit of buyer and seller. All the hotel groups now have their own sales departments and many of the large hotels carry out personal selling routines. The procedure is to research, plan, control and evaluate the activities as follows:

(a) *Determine what has to be sold*, the price and availability, and the factors influencing saleability — quality, location, differentiation.
(b) *Plan a programme* by identifying market and business sources — previous guests, visiting businessmen, travel agents, tourist boards, local societies, etc. This information can be obtained from the market analysis.
(c) *Prepare a sales call*, which can take the form of:
    identifying the decision-maker
    identifying the objective of the call
    thanking the interviewee for past business
    describing the product and its benefits
    using visual aids
    asking for business
    introducing and suggesting factors which can be considered at a follow-up call.
(d) *Record the interview* on record cards, to develop the relationship, by linking up past business with future expectations.

### Summary
The success of personal selling in obtaining new and repeat business has been proved by many firms, and possibly results from the fact that this form of selling allows the buyer to:

(i) communicate and exchange

(ii) learn from the salesman
(iii) identify the organisation directly
(iv) be persuaded.

## In-house selling

All employees who are in direct contact with customers should be made aware of the importance of selling services and products in order to utilise all the facilities of the unit, and consequently increase profits and provide a satisfactory experience for the guests.

Staff should be trained so that they have:

(a) a good knowledge of the products and services being offered
(b) an awareness that customers like to be greeted in a friendly manner and helped with their problems
(c) the ability to promote and sell

By being aware of the possible needs and wants of guests they will be able to make positive selling suggestions to:

(a) a traveller who may need his suit pressing
(b) tourists who may require breakfast in bed after a long journey
(c) parents who want a different meal for their children
(d) guests wanting a particular meal for health reasons, or the fact that they are in a hurry
(e) guests requiring a drink to accompany a meal.

### Summary

By showing concern for the guests the staff promote sales and increase the effectiveness of the unit.

## (ii)   Advertising

Advertising has been defined as paid for messages, describing the business in a favourable way by using posters, newspapers, television, radio, direct mail and magazines.

It is generally accepted that personal selling is the most effective form of promoting sales, but in the hotel and catering industry, where consumers make infrequent visits to hotels and come from a wide geographical area, it is obviously difficult and too costly to contact personally all potential buyers. Advertising is therefore an economic substitute for direct selling.

### The role of advertising

Advertisements should convey messages which will influence consumer attitudes and behaviour favourable to the seller with three objectives in mind.

(a) to increase immediate sales
(b) to make people aware of your existence
(c) to create a favourable image of the firm, over a long period of time.

73

To achieve the objectives, the messages conveyed:

(a) will sell the benefits a consumer will receive from a visit to a certain unit
(b) will highlight the product differences from those of competition
(c) inform and remind people of the organisation's existence and the suitability of its locations
(d) persuade potential consumers that they can expect good standards of services and suitable facilities.

### The selection of media
The selection of media should be based on the:

(a) objectives of the campaign
(b) market segments aimed at
(c) the characteristics of the individual medium.

Though media scheduling requires the skills of the media planners, it is reasonable for management to ask agents to justify their selection. Beside headcounting, an agent will make allowances if a particular media has repeat readership, or is a direct line to heavy users of a particular product or people considered to be innovators or opinion leaders. Assessments have to be made on the relative impact of newspapers, weekly or daily magazines, posters or radio; also colour, timing, front or back pages. As mentioned earlier, the work of an advertising agent can make promotion campaigns more cost effective, because of their specialised knowledge.

### Details of media

### Word-of-mouth advertising
A capable host can encourage personal advertising by the interest, attention and satisfaction he gives to guests, who in turn will recommend the hotel or come back themselves.

### Newspaper advertising
This form of advertising is particularly effective in attracting tourists and promoting food and beverage sales. A market analysis will show where the present guests are coming from, and this will suggest areas which may be developed. This form of advertising is flexible as it can be directed to particular areas, and response rates can be recorded by coding replies.

### Magazine advertising
Magazine advertising is becoming increasingly important in attracting people who wish to take part in activities while on holiday — fishing, bridge, climbing etc. It is a useful way of directing messages to the most potential market segments.

**Radio and television**

The individual owner manager has found television too costly. Specialised use of radio, particularly to the under 30 year old looking for a 'different' place to wine and dine has been very effective.

## (iii)   Direct mail

This form of advertising has many important features and has proved to be very effective in attracting new business and reminding previous guests of your continued existence.

The main advantages of direct mail are that you are able to:

(a) *select potential customers* who are likely to be interested in the services you offer. For example, target groups can be broken down into: geographical locations, leisure interests, industrial classifications and socio-economic groups
This makes direct mail very cost effective compared with other media
(b) *express a personal message* to each potential customer, which often means a higher response rate which will be more noticeable than the hundreds of other messages transmitted each day by other media
(c) *time the promotion* to link in with when decisions are taken or to relate to special occasions
(d) *measure accurately the responses* from various segments of the market and evaluate its cost effectiveness
(e) *make it an effective part of a multi-media campaign*

**Brochures**

Inquiries made through successful advertising will usually lead to a brochure being sent. A brochure is the best way of informing potential customers about a place. It can be read at leisure and be passed on to anyone interested. This consequently presents the opportunity to describe the hotel by words and photographs plus the additional advantage of providing information about the location, entertainment and amenities in the area.

**Summary**

Advertising informs and persuades potential consumers to the mutual benefits of buyer and seller.

## (iv)   Sales promotion

This has been described as those activities, controlled directly by the organisation or firm, which are used to develop sales over a short period of time.

The promotions are usually arranged to:

(a) encourage consumers to use a new hotel, restaurant, product or service
(b) appeal to a special segment of the market, eg week-end breaks for theatre goers in London

(c)  encourage sales during the off-peak periods, eg holidays for old age pensioners during April and October

(d)  compete with other units who are cutting prices

(e)  create a new type of trade, eg conferences for businessmen.

The activities which can be identified as sales promotion include:

(a)  *special prices* at particular times or to particular people

(b)  *special quantity rates* for block holiday bookings

(c)  *coupon offers* — collecting packet tops for a free meal at a particular restaurant

(d)  *free wine* -- with meals purchased on Monday and Tuesday, slow periods of trade

(e)  *free meals for children* — to encourage Sunday lunches.

**Summary**
Sales promotions are useful to attract new customers and increase the use of facilities over a short period of time.

Promotions however, if used too often can create intense competition and consumers will sometimes wait until special prices are offered, thus disrupting normal trade.

**Example of costing a sales promotion**
A 100 bedroom hotel in Herefordshire with a 40% occupancy rate for April offered a tour operator 30 bedrooms for two weeks for £50 per room. (The normal charge for two weeks was £100.)

The increased revenue amounted to £1500, plus extra sales in the bar and restaurant.

The only additional expenses were laundry and room service £300. (Breakfast was an extra charge.)

The fixed costs of administration, rates, insurance, etc, remained fixed and absorbed by the normal trade. Consequently the promotion increased profits by approximately £1,200.

Other benefits included:

(a)  the continued use of hotel staff

(b)  the possibility of the guests in the tour party returning or promoting the hotel by 'word of mouth' advertising

The hotel management had to be sure that the guests belonging to the tour party were not too unalike in appearance to and in their behaviour towards guests normally using the hotel.

## (v)  Merchandising
Merchandising includes all activities to increase sales, that take place within the unit. The objectives are:

(a)  encouraging guests to use all the facilities within the unit

(b)  influencing people so that they will return again.

To achieve the objectives merchandising must be planned to:

(a) encourage guests to make purchases 'on impulse', by making sure that they are aware of the presence of a product or service
(b) complete the vital link in a chain of activities leading to a purchase. A guest may have seen an advertisement for a product, but, a purchase can only be made at the 'point of sale'
(c) provide a service which will create a memorable experience.

Merchandising relies on attracting the attention of a guest and creating and developing interest and desire at the 'point of sale'. The methods used are numerous, here are a few examples.

| | |
|---|---|
| *Display materials* | Tent cards, posters, drink mats, menus, lighted pictures. |
| | Elevator cards, food and drink displays |
| *Display of skills* | Visual food preparation and bar service. |

**Summary**
Merchandising has the advantage of being related directly with the customer so actions and responses can be observed and controlled.

## (vi)   Public relations (PR)
*'Public relations is the deliberate, planned and sustained effort to establish mutual understanding between an organisation and its public'.*
*Institutue of Public Relations*

The purpose of public relations is to enchance the image of a firm so as to create a favourable attitude within the minds of the public. To do this, a two-way system of communication has to be established to develop mutual interests and understanding, based on knowledge presented by an organisation and an appreciation of peoples' needs, wants and desires.

*A system of public relations*

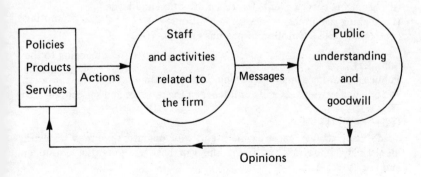

The public, a firm will wish to influence, covers the present and future:

— employees
— customers
— shareholders
— financial institutions
— government departments
— suppliers.

Creating favourable relationships with employees, by respecting them as individuals, involving them in the planning and formulation of standards, will influence the way in which staff will help and treat guests. In turn the guests will respond favourably if they are noticed, greeted and respected within an environment noted for its ethical standards, cleanliness and efficiency, which helps to satisfy the needs to feel safe and secure while away from home.

Shareholders, financial institutions, government departments and suppliers will react positively and show preference to an organisation which keeps them informed on policy and future developments and shows a social responsibility to the community.

The public relations activities are aimed at developing:

— internal relations
— external relations
— goodwill
— sales of products and services.

The activities include:

(a) arranging company meetings for managers to explain policy and to receive ideas and suggestions
(b) involvement in dispersing information through company magazines, newsletters and educational films
(c) involvement with the affairs of the local community
(d) maintaining relationships with journalists, to encourage the publication of developments and events
(e) arranging special events to attract attention and trade
(f) making the arrangements for exhibitions
(g) support the promotion of products and services.

## Summary
Public relations is a technique which helps to build a company's reputation, and create an awareness and confidence in the product and services offered.

## (vii) Agents
Trade associations, travel agencies and tour operators are now becoming increasingly important in filling the gap between potential consumers and hotels.

People are changing their holiday habits. The growth of education, increases in disposable wealth, the development of promotional techniques, more cars, are all encouraging people to seek new places and indeed new types of holidays. The one or two weeks by the sea is now less popular and the alternatives require more organisation as people wish to engage in special activities or be with tourists with similar interests as themselves.

Several organisations will now provide the choice and expertise in booking holidays which will reduce anxiety and satisfy the emotional and psychological needs of security, safety, belongingness and self-realisation.

Consequently promotion through travel agents, tour operators, tourist boards, etc, can be beneficial to meet a changing market demand.

## 3 Re-opening The Chiltern Hotel — a case study

The promotion of The Chiltern Hotel in the past was considered to be inappropriate for the future.

Consequently the management decided to have two separate promotional plans.

Plan I — General promotion
Plan II — A special promotion plan for the items outlined in the marketing plan

**Note**
The items for Plan I are described in detail, but the details for Plan II, are to be built up by the student.

# Activities

---
## 1 Formulating promotion plans

### Promotion — Plan I
In order to successfully promote the re-opening of The Chiltern Hotel and its service, it was thought essential to divide the facilities into two departments:

(a) accommodation
(b) restaurant

Catering for a national and local need respectively.

Concerning the restuarant, it was thought that advertising should begin eight days prior to the opening day, which itself would be split between lunch and evening trade.

| | |
|---|---|
| *Lunchtime:* | Invitation cards would be sent to local dignitaries and firms' representatives offering a buffet lunch with drinks free of charge. This would create an awareness of new ownership. |
| *Evening:* | A traditional menu would be offered, together with a free bottle of wine to each table in the restaurant. |

With both functions, it would be essential that all the hotel facilities offered would be operational; providing satisfaction to curious customers. Promotional extras, such as pens, need also to be visible, these enable further advertising to be made once the item has left the hotel.

Brochures would have to be given to each customer upon leaving so enabling them to be passed on to friends wishing to perhaps dine or stay in the district.

Concerning accommodation, a short-list was complied to provide maximum benefit concerning advertising.

| | | |
|---|---|---|
| 1 | *Direct Mail to local firms* | To make aware to businessmen the Chiltern Hotel and its tariff, enabling companies to recommend the hotel |
| 2 | *AA/RAC* | Applying for membership would eventually, after six months, provide advertising in the Motoring guide books, and a rating for the hotel which would assist travellers looking for accommodation in a particular category |
| 3 | *BHRCA* | This association also provides additional advertising and other benefits for the hotel member. One such example is the transfer of surplus customers to a hotel in the association not having 100% bedroom occupancy. |

| | | |
|---|---|---|
| 4 | *Yellow pages* | Would-be clients arriving in the district with no accommodation already booked would use a Yellow Pages directory for assistance |
| 5 | *A taxi firm* | As with (4), clients frequently ask the advice of taxi drivers. A business arrangement with a particular taxi firm would decide whether The Chiltern Hotel gave the cabs business if they provided some of the customers. |

Concerning the restaurant, a further list was drawn up.

| | | |
|---|---|---|
| 1 | *Local press* | feature articles and 'Dining out' coverage needs to be operated by local papers such as the Manchester Evening News and the Guardian series, so that prospective customers know what to expect in the restaurant with regard to the type, price and atmosphere. |
| 2 | *Yellow pages* | provide quick reference to restaurant establishments |
| 3 | *Parochial magazines* | will mainly attract the people in church unions interested in using the afternoon tea facilities to accommodate groups for annual meetings. Such groups would be Mothers' Union, Young Wives, who in turn may bring their husbands along for an evening meal |
| 4 | *Life magazines* | these books are famous for their reference to good dining establishments in the Cheshire or Lancashire regions |
| 5 | *Taxis* | as with the accommodation comment, taxi drivers frequently advise on the spot, places where one can dine, to a stranger new in the area |
| 6 | *Posters* | provide advertising in strategic points, such as railway stations and bus depots. |

## Brochure

**Contents**
    External photograph
    Internal photographs
    Description of facilities
    Style and type of rooms
    Location with a small diagrammatical map
    Statement of any specific restrictions
    Special functions available, eg Edwardian evening

## Layout of brochure

**Front page**
    External photograph
    Name of establishment
    Address and telephone number of establishment
    Name of proprietor

**Inside**
    Internal photographs with a brief description of each
    Include — dining room, lounge, bar, bedroom
    Mention any special functions, what they consist of and their frequency
    State all tariffs on a loose page, which could be replaced, when necessary

**Back page**
    Diagrammatical location map showing the hotel's position in relation
    to surrounding towns: Manchester
                              Altrincham
                                Chester
                                Manchester airport

State any specific restrictions applicable to the hotel.

## Hotel motif

To use for internal advertising, a motif can be used as a symbol for the hotel. In this case, a suitable motif may be a diagrammatical line drawing of the hotel exterior, viewed from the side.

Certain items may be used in the hotel for their advertising qualities, for example, book matches which may be removed by the guest and passed round so spreading the name of the hotel.

## Bedrooms

The items which may be used in this area, with ideas of how they may advertise the hotel, are as follows:

### 1 Notepads

White paper notepads with the following:
Black printed motif in top right hand corner
Black printed name, address, phone number of the hotel in top left/ central area.

### 2 Pencils/pens

Ordinary white pens and pencils with the name of the hotel printed in black.

### 3 Mending sets

Styled like large books of matches. Inside the leaf a brief description of the hotel and its facilities.
The book to be white in colour with the following black printing:
The hotel motif and name
The mending sets should contain
black cotton
white cotton
2 needles
2 safety pins

### 4 Ashtrays

Round glass ashtrays with a central black motiff and the hotel name semi-circled under the motif.

## Dining-room

The following items for use in the dining room have been decided in certain colours which may, of course, need changing depending on the final décor (dark green and gold) of the room.

### 1 Drink coasters

Green, circular, card coasters with a central gold motif.

### 2 Ashtrays

Dark green, round glass ashtrays with a thin gold edging and a central gold mctif.

### 3 Mint envelopes

Dark green in colour with the name of the hotel and its address/phone number printed in gold.

## Bar

As the bar is likely to have a variety of customers it is a good idea to have items that may be removed from the hotel and shown to friends, eg, sale of book matches.

### 1 Drink coasters
Coasters of the paper type. White in colour with a dark blue central motif printed with the name of the hotel semi-circled underneath this.

### 2 Ashtrays
Round, glass ashtrays with the motif printed centrally in dark blue, with the hotel name underneath.

### 3 Book matches
Blue background with the name, address and phone number of the hotel printed in white. Possibly a brief description of the hotel and its facilities inside the leaf.

### General Areas

### 1 Business cards
White cards printed with the
  — name of the proprietor
  -- name, address and phone number of the hotel.

### 2 Bill books
Showing the hotel motif
  name of the proprietor
  name, address and phone number of the hotel.

### 3 Letter heads
For use in all correspondence, to guests, suppliers and all contacts. Set out in the same way as the notepads found in the guests' bedrooms.

### 4 Skeleton menus and wine lists
Printed with motif, name of proprietor and hotel address and phone number. Giving lists of the menu offered and the wines for sale. This is to be sent out to customers on their request.

## Promotion — Plan II — The Chiltern Hotel

The work of researching, analysing and profit planning has been completed and we are confident that if the firm:

(a) kept to the cost and profit margins normally accepted by hotel operators
(b) developed sales which would utilise some of our under-used resources outlined in the marketing plan, the unit could become a profitable organisation.

Promotion is the key to success and we have to organise our promotional activities to increase:

(a) the occupancy rates, by developing the November to April, the week-end, and the transient tourists trade from the airport
(b) the number of lunch-time customers, having changed the menu, service and atmosphere for mid-day
(c) the 'special occasion' trade — wedding receptions and anniversaries.

This would be done by:

1 persuading a prospective customer to use our hotel
2 giving him a service, so that:
    (a) he will spend the maximum amount on our services and facilities
    (b) he will return
    (c) the establishment will be 'sold' by word-of-mouth advertising.

The hotel used:    Personal selling
                      Advertising
                      Direct mail
                      Merchandising — internal selling
                      Public relations and general publicity

---

Design a promotion plan for one year, taking into account:

(a) the market segments identified for the hotel
(b) the objectives within the market and profit plans
(c) how much should be spent
(d) the message and mode of presentation
(e) the media that should be used
(f) how advertising should be phrased throughout the year
(g) the best methods of measuring the effectiveness of the efforts.

The budget should contain an analysis of costs, and reasons for the decisions you have made.

Note    A detailed analysis of the Chiltern Hotel and its environment is contained in Chapter III — Marketing Research

---

## 2   An in-depth study of advertising

### The Chiltern Hotel — Special occasion trade

**Report to the directors**
Having been asked to prepare a report upon the 'Special occasion' trade —
wedding receptions and anniversaries — it is presented here, in two main
sections, *viz:*

1   Analysis
2   The recommended marketing plan we should adopt.

**Section I**
A   *Product analysis*

1   The hotel is geographically well located for people travelling from
    various parts of the country
2   The hotel has a good parking area, image and facilities, compared with
    other hotels in the area
3   We need to use the facilities, particularly during the week-end, when
    trade declines as businessmen return home.

B   *Market analysis*

1   The area within five miles of the hotel contains 39,000 people from the
    'A' and 'B' socio-economic groups who can afford 'special occasions'
2   The local papers during the year shows a *weekly* average of 45 'Special
    Occasions' within ten miles of the hotel, as the hotel only had during
    the year, 20 parties, much of this trade went to competitors.

C   *Financial analysis*

1   The charges made by the hotel were very high and had VAT and a 10%
    service charge added to them. We found that the previous owners
    allowed an outside caterer to organise each function and keep the
    proceeds for a payment of £10 for each event.
2   This type of trade was very profitable as the food costs were usually
    30% rather than 45% for ordinary meals. Also the sale of drinks provided
    a considerable increase to normal profits.

It is estimated that 20 special events last year, produced the following results:

|  | Food | | Liquor | | Total | |
|---|---|---|---|---|---|---|
|  | £ | % | £ | % | £ | % |
| Sales | 1800 | 100 | 1000 | 100 | 2800 | 100 |
| Cost of sales | 600 | 30 | 500 | 50 | 1100 | 35 |
| Wages | 600 | 30 | 100 | 10 | 700 | 25 |
| Contribution | 600 | 40 | 400 | 40 | 1000 | 40 |

### Note
Fixed costs have not been included as they are absorbed by the normal trade of the hotel.

### Section II
*The marketing plan*
1 Long-term objectives

(a) to promote and expand the Special Occasion trade, as it could bring additional business to the hotel
(b) to control the events from within the hotel, rather than give the work to an outside caterer
(c) to obtain 100 special occasions during the coming year.

2 Short-term objectives

(a) produce new menus andprices, without extra charges
(b) to promote mainly in the local weekly press
(c) analyse competitors' prices and activities.

Present a promotion plan for increasing this type of trade and include suggestions for the:

(a) message
(b) media
(c) market
(d) cost
(e) expected profit for the year

## A Student project

Effective communication does not happen simply by committing large amounts of money to media advertising. Without research and planning a large advertising budget can be totally wasted.

A catering unit has to decide what *target audience* it wishes to reach, the *best media* to use, what features of the product/service will appeal and what type of message would be most suitable. These factors have to be taken into account to link with a marketing task which could be to:

(a) increase sales
(b) create interest
(c) increase awareness

(d) maintain market share
(e) inform the customer
(f) re-assure.

### Stage I

Collect one copy of
- a local daily or weekly newspaper
- a popular daily newspaper
- a serious daily newspaper
- a magazine.

### Questions

1 Determine the circulation and advertising rates for each media.
2 Briefly describe the type of people you feel each media aims to attract for its readership.

### Stage II

Cut out six advertisements related to hotel, catering and tourism.

Run an experiment with other students to see which advertisements are most frequently remembered by exposing each one to each student for five seconds in turn.

1 Describe:
(a) why some advertisements are easily remembered and others not
(b) what the objectives of the advertisements are
(c) the market segments aimed at
(d) communication principles used, eg
  - rational argument
  - emotional appeal
  - comparative results

2 Compare and contrast advertising in newspapers and magazines with radio, television, posters and cinemas.

**Stage III**

**Case study**                    **Chiltern restaurant**

**Financial results of 1981**

|                    |         | £        |
| ------------------ | ------- | -------- |
| No of covers       |         | 100,000  |
| Sales — ASP        |         | 3        |
| Sales - Total      |         | 300,000  |
| Fixed costs        | 144,000 |          |
| Variable costs     | 120,000 |          |
| Total costs        |         | 264,000  |
| Profit             |         | 36,000   |

**Objectives of advertising campaign — for the coming year**

(a)  to increase the ASP from £3 to £3.50
(b)  to increase sales by 10%

**Strategy**

(a)  to increase drink sales during the meal
(b)  to advertise evening trade, Friday and Saturday.

Estimated advertising cost £5,000

**Present a budget based on the objectives described above**

---

## 3    Self-assessment questions

After working through the study material and text books test your knowledge.

1  How do you achieve effectiveness in advertising?
2  How would you describe advertising?
3  What is sales promotion?
4  Define public relations
5  Describe the differences between internal and external selling

## 4    Test V

1 Describe the type of promotional mix that may be used in a large hotel. Explain how you would identify the market area at which to aim your promotional campaign

2 Outline the major media alternatives available to a publicity manager. What steps should he take to plan a campaign?

3 You have been asked to design a promotion campaign for a restaurant. What kinds of research might you carry out before deciding on the correct media

4 Describe four main methods of determining the size of the promotion budget and comment on their limitations

5 Write explanatory notes on the following:

(i)   Public relations

(ii)  Sales promotions

(iii) Merchandising

(iv)  Personal selling

# VI
# Pricing

**Areas of study**
1 The factors involved in pricing decisions
2 Pricing methods in the hotel and catering industry

**Objectives**
On completing this chapter and case studies the reader should be able to:

(a) describe the factors influencing pricing decisions
(b) differentiate between the various pricing methods used in the industry eg
(i) cost plus
(ii) differential profit margins
(iii) contribution pricing
(iv) pricing based on return on investment
(c) analyse the relationships between costs, competition, and market forces to pricing decisions.

**Case studies and activities**
1 Case study I — Cost-plus pricing
2 Case study II — The use of contribution pricing
3 Case study III — Return on investment pricing and market forces
4 Self-assessment questions
5 Test VI

**Readings**
GILES, *Marketing*, Chapter V
KOTAS, *Marketing Orientation*, Chapter II

**Pricing**

The catering establishments which are linked to the welfare, industrial and educational sectors are usually cost orientated, and pricing is based to recover the expenses set within a budget. Hotels and restaurants in the commercial sector are market orientated and design their products and prices to meet market needs and provide a profit.

Pricing is the last critical factor of the marketing process:

 — products can be designed to suit markets
 - promotion can persuade and inform.

But, unless the price is acceptable to a sufficiently large enough market for the seller to make a profit, the marketing process has failed.

In the hotel and catering industry there are many ways in which prices are arrived at, and , even within the same organisation or unit, one can find different policies and methods, for example:

 - the selling price of a double room may be arrived at by accepting the charges fixed by a competitor
 - the selling price of a bottle of wine may not have any relationship to cost, but, is set at what the market will accept
 — the food cost of a meal may be considered to be 40%, and therefore the selling price is 100%.

## 1 The factors involved in pricing decisions

(a) The characteristics of the product
(b) Company policy
(c) The characteristics of the market
(d) Competition
(e) Cost characteristics.

*Diagram showing factors influencing pricing decisions*

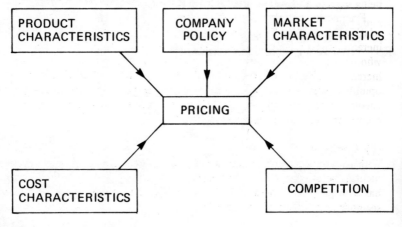

**(a)  The characteristics of the product**
Though products should be designed to satisfy demand, customers are often prepared to pay extra if the product has selected differences, a market uniqueness which cannot be found easily elsewhere. This also embraces the 'snob appeal' of some places where the patrons believe they can gather together in splendid isolation.

Each product however has a life cycle, and though a new craze or venture may be able to attract a higher price to begin with, eventually the selling price may be reduced to normal levels.

**(b)  Company policy**
The philosopnhy of the firm, its objectives and desired image must be taken into account when fixing a price. A low priced poor quality product could damage the image and reputation of the firm needlessly. In the catering industry, many caterers prefer to compete through product differentiation directed at particular target segments.

But, over a period of one year or more, prices should reflect the company objectives, which could be one or more of the following:

(i)   to maximise profit, relevant to a product with a short product life cycle
(ii)  to achieve a target return on investment
(iii) to stabilise prices, to build up goodwill
(iv)  to make it difficult for competitors to enter the market
(v)   to follow the brand leader in pricing
(vi)  to increase the market or maintain market share.

**(c)  The characteristics of the market**
Price is an important device in helping a caterer to promote and appeal to particular segments of the market which he feels will be suitable for his product. The consumers will naturally see a price as a reflection of the quantity and quality of the food, décor, variety, service, atmosphere, etc, being offered and will be disappointed if their expectations are not satisfied.

Frequently catering operations have to consider 'price elasticity', the relative sensitivity of a product's sales volume to a change in price. A small increase in the price of a meal at lunch-time can be important to consumers who eat out regularly and they could look for another supplier, while an increase in the price of an evening meal will have little effect on consumers' opinions, who eat out occasionally. Seasonal factors in the industry can encourage different prices to be charged at different times of the year or even within one week, eg mini-week-ends.

**(d)  Competition**
With the reduction of product life cycles brought about through environmental factors and consumers' eagerness to accept something new, watch has to be kept on prices and competitors' activities to prevent the market segment moving out of your market.

**(e) Cost characteristics**

Cost plays a part in any pricing situation, because at the end of the day the company's costs must be covered.

What the marketing manager seeks is flexibility in fixing prices, so as:

(i)   to attract more customers to use certain facilities at certain times of the week, month or year
(ii)  to discourage competitors
(iii) to develop trade within particular markets — conferences, functions etc
(iv)  to adjust to changes in technology which affect cost patterns, eg convenience foods.

## 2 Pricing methods in the hotel and catering industry

### Cost-plus pricing

In many catering establishments, it is agreed that the food cost should be a certain percentage of price paid for the meal.

For example if the policy of the catering unit, was for the food cost to be 40%, then 60% would go towards paying wages and fixed overheads and providing a profit margin

If the food cost of a dish was 80p which is 40%;

$$\text{the selling price would be} = \frac{80}{1} \times \frac{100}{40} = £2.00.$$

The advantages of the method is that it is easy to calculate, but, it does not take into account differences in the preparation and cooking times between dishes.

### Differential gross profit-pricing for menus

To make allowances for preparation and cooking time and react to the market, it is more desirable to have different mark-up percentages for different items, eg soup and vegetables could have a mark-up of 70% while fish 50%.

This could have the effect of reducing the price of a main dish compared to competitors and reflect the low preparation time for fish and the large amount of preparation time needed for vegetables and soup.

| Menu items | Food cost | Differential GP % | Selling price |
|---|---|---|---|
| Soup | 0.21p | 70 | 0.70 |
| Fish | 1.00 | 50 | 2.00 |
| Vegetables | 0.35 | 70 | 1.20 |
| Sweet | 0.48 | 60 | 1.20 |
| | £2.04 | (60) | £5.10 |

### Contribution pricing

Contribution pricing is a technique used to develop particular markets and increase sales and profits. It is assumed that the sales expected and budgeted for, are recovering the fixed costs, and therefore any additional sales can be priced to recover materials and direct labour, plus a margin which contributes to the profits. This means that under-utilised facilities can be used by having an attractive price. More and more hotels are using this promotional tactic to encourage conferences, functions, week-end trade and out of season holidays.

## Rate of return on investment pricing

This method is aimed at providing a net profit which is related to the capital used in the business.

For example if £100,000 was used to buy a restaurant it would be reasonable to expect 15% net profit, eg £15,000.

The fixed costs, rent depreciation, salaries etc are then estimated or calculated from known figures, the sales are then estimated, and consequently by determing the food costs, eg 30% to 45% the required net profit can be budgeted for.

In the example below fixed costs for the year were estimated to be £165,000.

Sales turnover was expected to be 300,000 covers a year at £1.

Then the food cost would be:

|  | £ |
|---|---|
| Sales 300,000 covers @ £1 | 300,000 |
| Less food cost (40%) | 120,000 |
| Profit-gross | 180,000 |
| Less fixed expenses | 165,000 |
| NET PROFIT | 15,000 |

As Kotas states in his book *Management Accounting for Hotels and Restaurants*, this method shows:

'the direct link between prices, profit margins and the capital of the business. However, it ignores more factors influencing prices than it takes into account, namely the customer and market demand'

## Summary

Price setting involves the consideration of many aspects of the business, the product, market, competition, company policy and costs, but in the long-term prices must be set that:

(a) are acceptable to the public
(b) recover costs and provide a surplus/profit
(c) meet budget requirements in the welfare sector of the industry *or*
   — recover costs and provide a surplus/profit in the commercial sector of the industry.

It is sometimes acceptable for an organisation to vary prices to promote and encourage business, but in the long-term the two objectives stated above must be achieved.

## Case studies and activities

As price setting is an important activity for every catering manager, it is hoped that the following case studies will lead to a greater understanding by enabling the reader:

(a) to set prices himself
(b) to compare his decisions with what actually happened in the industry.

Case study I — deals with cost plus pricing and differential profit margins.

Case study II — considers the use of contribution pricing.

Case study III — deals with the need to consider the return on capital when setting prices, together with market factors.

# Activities

### 1  Case study I — cost-plus pricing at The Chiltern Hotel

The Chiltern Hotel decided to develop meals at lunch-time, which would be aimed at the upper end of the 'pub grub' market. The objectives were to increase profits and to utilise unused production facilities at lunch-time. It was also thought that customers using the hotel at lunch-time would be encouraged to return in the evening.

The estimated sales were based on competitors' activities and the chef costed out certain dishes with the following results.

|  | Cost per portion pence | Expected weekly sales (portions) |
|---|---|---|
| Soup | 10 | 250 |
| Hot pot | 35 | 300 |
| Cheese/Onion pie | 30 | 200 |
| Vegetables | 10 | 400 |
| Sweets | 15 | 400 |
| Coffee | 8 | 500 |

The estimated wage costs of two part-timers — £160 per week
Fixed overhead — rent, fuel, promotion etc — £65 per week

## A market research report on the situation

### Findings

1 It was usually the practice to price food in hotels by taking the cost of food to equal 40% (60% GP) and make the selling price 100%
2 The main competition in the area was selling 'meat pies at 60p', they were produced in a local bakery and served hot at the bar-counter on a paper plate, without cutlery.
3 The primary market would be women shoppers and office workers and a survey suggested strong support for coffee and a sweet. The secondary market would be businessmen, and they expressed a preference for soup and a hot dish.

### Recommendations

The type of customer likely to use the establishment at lunch-time, suggested that:

(a) good cutlery and crockery should be used
(b) individual servings would be wanted
(c) word of mouth advertising would be more beneficial than heavy promotion and advertising, this suggested the use of product differentiation to stimulate a talking point.

### What do you think?

Consider the report and the information presented and suggest:

(a) prices to be charged:

(b) estimated weekly profit:

(c) a product image and sales promotion:

**Solution to the case study on cost plus pricing**

**Introduction**
It was pointed out to the management that *cost plus pricing*, though used more than any other method in the industry, ignored:

(a) customers' expectations, needs and wants
(b) competition
(c) return on investment
(d) the labour and energy content of each item on the menu, eg the cost of preparing vegetables is far more than preparing soup or coffee

Differential profit margins, which is a variation on cost plus pricing, could be applied to the different items on the menu, which could take into account cost factors, promotional aspects and competition.

**Decisions taken**
After considering all the data, the management decided that:

(a) differential gross profit margins should be set for each item in the menu.
(i) to try and lower prices against the competition coming from the meat pies
(ii) to reflect the work content in the vegetables and sweets, preparation costs were high, compared with the soup
(iii) to promote the value for money aspect — less than usual would be charged for coffee
(b) individual portions of the hot pot and cheese and onion pie were prepared, cooked and served in individual earthenware pots
(c) the image of home prepared foods was to be generated and the use of Cheshire cheese, and Cheshire beef in the main products.

*Weekly estimated trading results — using differential profit margins*

| Item | Cost price p | No | Total cost £ | Cost % | DPM % | Sales value £ | Selling price p |
|------|------|-----|--------|--------|-------|---------|---------|
| Soup | 10 | 250 | 25.00 | 40 | 60 | 62.50 | 25 |
| Cheshire hot pot | 35 | 300 | 105.00 | 50 | 50 | 210.00 | 70 |
| Cheshire cheese pie | 30 | 200 | 60.00 | 40 | 60 | 150.00 | 75 |
| Vegetables | 10 | 400 | 40.00 | 25 | 75 | 160.00 | 40 |
| Sweets | 15 | 400 | 60.00 | 30 | 70 | 200.00 | 50 |
| Coffee | 8 | 500 | 40.00 | 67 | 33 | 53.00 | 12 |
| | | | 330.00 | 40 | 60 | 835.50 | |

|  | £ |
|--|--|
| Estimated weekly sales — | 835.50 |
| Less food costs (approx 40%) | 330.00 |
| Gross profit (60%) | 505.50 |
| Less wages £160 | |
| Less fixed expenses £65 | 225.00 |
| Estimated weekly net profit | 280.00 |
| Estimated yearly net profit — £14,000 | |

Estimated yearly net profit — £14,000

**What actually happened**

1 The lunch sales, after six months reached £800 a week, the costs, due to inflation, reached a total of £600 (including food, wages and over-heads) giving the company an additional £10,000 profit in one financial year.
2 The two main market segments, turned out to be:
(a) businessmen, usually on expense accounts
(b) women office workers and shoppers.
3 The women expressed a desire for salads, which were added to the menu shortly after the opening.

## 2 Case study II -- The use of contribution pricing in developing sales in a hotel restaurant

**Introduction**
Over the past three years The Chiltern Hotel restaurant had been operating without change for seven nights a week. It is a medium sized restaurant with a maximum capacity of 100 covers, the take-up level of which has been approximately 25%.

The company directors expressed concern about the large amount of space which was not revenue earning, particularly at week-ends.

**Action by management**
The management decided to analyse the situation, with the view to improving the sales and profits. The expected results for the present year are shown in the profit plan below:

#### The restaurant profit plan

|  | Food (not including drink sales) |
|---|---|
|  | £ |
| Estimated sales | 42,500 |
| Less cost of food sold | 17,000 |
| GROSS PROFIT | 25,500 |
| Less wages and £17,500 | |
| fixed expenses 5,000 | 22,500 |
| Net profit (before tax) | 3,000 |

The analysis took the form of:
(a) observing the restaurant operations and customers for two weeks
(b) interpreting the statistics available
(c) carrying out a survey to ascertain the type of meals that would appeal to the customers using the hotel at the week-end.

Results of the surveys

### A   Observations of the restaurant

This survey showed that:

(i)  the restaurant was particularly under-used at the week-end, while at the same time the bar areas were full.

(ii) that the customers from Monday to Thursday were mainly middle-aged businessmen.

(iii) at the week-end, Friday to Sunday the main customers were under 40, and from their dress, drinking habits, and cars they reflected a feeling of having above average disposable wealth.

| Customers using bar/restaurant | | |
|---|---|---|
| | **Monday-Thursday** | **Friday-Sunday** |
| Age | Mainly above 40 | Mainly below 40 |
| Social position | On their own | In groups |
| Dress | Formal | Informal |
| Drinking habits | Average and below | High level of expenditure |
| Influencing factor in choice of food | — Main meal of the day<br>— Time unimportant<br>— On expense account | To socialise |

### B   Statistical analysis

(i)  *Population census*    — the hotel was situated in an area which contained a high concentration of well-paid people.
       — *Percentage of employers, managers and professional workers:*
          Cheshire county        — 14.9%
          Area of hotel           — 32.1%

(ii) *Analysis of food sales showed:*

| | **Breakfast** | **Evening meal** | **Total** |
|---|---|---|---|
| Sales receipts | £10,000 | £32,500 | £42,500 |

(iii) *Number of covers in the evening*

| Mon | Tues | Wed | Thurs | Fri | Sat | Sun |
|-----|------|-----|-------|-----|-----|-----|
| 30 | 38 | 40 | 32 | 7 | 10 | 5 |

(iv) *Estimated weekly profit and loss account*

|  |  | Dinner | Breakfast |
|---|---|---|---|
|  |  | £ | £ |
| Estimated weekly receipts |  | 648 | 200 |
| Less estimated food costs (40%) |  | 259 | 80 |
| GROSS PROFIT |  | 389 | 120 |
| Total GP |  | 509 |  |
| Less wage cost | 350 |  |  |
| Less fixed expenses | 100 | 450 |  |
| Weekly estimated net profit |  | 59 |  |

## C  Market survey

This survey was an attempt to identify the needs and wants of the people using the hotel, particularly in the bar, during the week-end. The survey was conducted in the hotel and valid replies were obtained from seventy-three people, who were interviewed and asked to rate factors of preference against a scale of A to E.

| Influencing factor | Identification of need |
|---|---|
| Menu | Number of courses |
| Style of service | Silver to self-service |
| Meal and drink | Meal supported by drink or |
|  | Drink supported by meal |
| Price | £5 to £1 |
| Atmosphere | High Class or bistro type |
| Drink | Wine or coffee |

The results showed a preference for:

(i)   one course meal
(ii)  waitress service
(iii) meal to be part of the evening out, not the main purpose of the evening
(iv)  price approximately £2
(v)   bistro atmosphere supported by wine.

From a list of five dishes, kebabs and pizza's ranked the highest, and several people expressed a wish to have an all inclusive price.

**Summary**
The details recorded showed two distinct markets with different needs and wants, which reflected:

(a) the situation in which the customers found themselves and,
(b) the difference in age, social, economic, cultural and psychological backgrounds.

It seemed to confirm the necessity of providing a different food service at the week-end to the one offered during the week.

**What do you think?**
Consider the reports and the information presented and suggest:

(a) the type of food service you would offer, relate your answer to price, product, promotion and profit margin
(b) the estimated profit, if the week-end trade reached 100 covers. It is estimated that additional wage costs would be 15% of sales value.

**Decisions taken**

It was decided to transfer at the week-end the main restaurant service for guests staying at the hotel to the lounge and use the restaurant for a new food service. Lighting and music would be used to create a different atmosphere. The staff would be students from a local catering college.

Pizza and kebabs would be served at the price of £2 — including VAT and service.

|  |  | £ |
|---|---|---|
| Selling price for each dish | = | 2.00 |
| Less VAT 15% of £1.74 |  | 0.26 |
| Selling price without VAT |  | 1.74 |

|  | £ |  |
|---|---|---|
| Food cost (50%) | 0.87 |  |
| Wage cost (15%) | 0.26 |  |
| Fixed costs* |  |  |
| Additional cost | 1.13 |  |
| Plus free glass of wine | 0.12 |  |
| Total |  | 1.25 |
| PROFIT |  | 0.49 |

**\*Note**

It was considered that the main restaurant recovered all the fixed costs and that this normal expense could be replaced by a free glass of wine to create a promotional talking point for customers.

**What actually happened**

1 The covers sold at the week-end reached 120 after six months, giving an additional profit as shown below.

|  |  | £ |
|---|---|---|
| Sales 120 covers @ £2 | = | 240.00 |
| Less 15% $= \dfrac{240}{115} \times \dfrac{100}{1}$ | = | 20.90 |
|  |  | 219.10 |

|  | £ |  |
|---|---|---|
| Food cost (50%) | 109.55 |  |
| Wage cost (15%) | 23.86 |  |
| Fixed cost | — | 147.81 |
| Free wine | 14.40 |  |
| Weekly additional net profit |  | 71.29 |

Approximately £3,500 per year.

2  By using the restaurant it left more space in the bar, providing a quicker service which seemed to attract more customers or allowed the present customers to drink more.

The increased sales of approximately £5,000 per year gave an additional profit of £2,500.

Therefore the change to include an additional food service increased profit of the unit by approximately £6,000 a year. It is difficult to estimate the value of offering free wine, but it obviously was popular. The appreciation of contribution pricing made it possible for the company to give something free to the customers because of the absence of fixed costs.

## 3  Case Study III — Return on investment pricing and market forces

In the hotel industry, more firms are seeing the necessity of working towards a rate of return on capital invested. This means that pricing decisions are made so that sales receipts cover all costs and provide a rate of return on the investment made. This case study involves a hotel which used the rate of return on investment as a guide, when setting prices, but, also considered:

(a)  what the market would pay
(b)  competitors' prices.

### Introduction
The directors of The Chiltern Hotel were anxious to consider the building of extra bedrooms.

The factors that had led to this interest were as follows:

(a)  present occupancy rates were increasing, the new motorway had attracted new business into the area and the international airport nearby attracted four million passengers each year
(b)  part of the present building could be used and land was available for an extension
(c)  extra guests would help to increase the profits of the food and beverages areas
(d)  the company had capital available and to invest it in buildings seemed a good hedge against inflation
(e)  the government anticipated a growth in tourism in the 1980s and gave a tax incentive to hotels building extensions of 12 bedrooms or more (Budget 1978).

### A joint report from a marketing consultant and architect
Plans were presented for 28 twin bedrooms, which gave the facilities which anticipated what businessmen and tourists would expect in the 1980s.

(i) Ensuite bathrooms for all bedrooms
(ii) Coffee/tea facilities in all rooms, with continental breakfast service
(iii) Telephone, radio and television in all rooms.

The extension also included a shop, which a local businessman wished to rent and would be used to sell sweets, tobacco, novelties, paintings and craftwork from local industries.

### Financial and statistical analysis

|  | £ |
|---|---|
| The estimated capital cost of converting part of the present building and constructing an extension including a shop area | 208,000 |
| Estimated capital cost of furniture and fittings for bedrooms | 65,000 |
| Design, surveyor and architect fees | 27,000 |
| TOTAL CAPITAL EXPENDITURE | 300,000 |
|  | £ |
| Yearly interest cost 15% | 45,000 |
| Yearly return on capital 15% | 45,000 |
| Required annual coverage | 90,000 |

Estimated charge per room based on required annual charge
1 Statistics from the Regional Tourist Board and a national marketing research organisation showed room occupancy rates for the area at 66%.
2 The figures available from internal records showed a split of double and single bookings of approximately 50:50.
3 That a reasonable occupancy rate would be 60%, split evenly between doubles and singles.

|  | Estimated room nights per year |
|---|---|
| 14 doubles with 60% single occupancy | 3,066 |
| 14 doubles with 60% double occupancy | 3,066 |
|  | 6,132 |

Estimated cost per room equals $= \dfrac{\text{annual coverage}}{\text{room nights}} = \dfrac{90{,}000}{6{,}132} = £14.7$

Plus a variable service cost of an estimated £2.00 per room
Plus VAT at 15%
Charge per room based on required annual charge $\qquad = £19.20$

The competition room rates — excluding breadfasts:

|  | Double £ | Single £ |
|---|---|---|
| An hotel | 33.00 | 24.00 |
| An airport hotel | 26.00 | 22.00 |
| A town hotel | 29.00 | 23.00 |

What do you think?

Consider the report and the information presented and suggest:

(a) prices that should be charged

(b) estimated yearly sales and the pay-back period.

Solutions to the case study

What actually happened

Management decided to charge £26 for a double and £21 for a single, after considering the market factors on return on investment. Prices would include VAT and continental breakfast.

Final calculations $\qquad\qquad\qquad\qquad\qquad$ £

Total estimated capital expenditure $\qquad\qquad$ 300,000

|  | £ |
|---|---|
| Yearly interest cost — 15% | 45,000 |
| Yearly return on capital 15% | 45,000 |
| Required annual coverage | 90,000 |

Estimated income and profit from rooms and shop

| Number | Type of occupancy |
|--------|-------------------|
| 14 | Single @ 60% |
| 14 | Double @ 60% |
| 28 | |

Plus estimated income from shop — 640 sq ft
at £3 per sq ft per year

(a) Period of payback — 6½ years
(b) Return on capital 21.8% before tax
(c) Return on capital 15.4% after tax

| Estimated room nights per year | Inclusive rate | £ |
|---|---|---|
| 3,066 | 21 | 64,386 |
| 3,066 | 26 | 79,716 |
| 6,132 | | 144,102 |
| Less VAT 15% | | 18,795 |
| | | 125,307 |
| Less Service cost @ £2 per room | | 12,264 |
| | | 113,043 |
| Less Continental Breakfast 50p per person | | 4,600 |
| | | 108,443 |
| | | 1,957 |
| | | 110,400 |
| Less interest on capital — 15% | | 45,000 |
| INCOME LESS INTEREST | | 65,400 |

| | | |
|---|---|---|
| Less tax | 65,400 | |
| Less allowance (see note below) | 5,900 | |
| TAXABLE INCOME | 49,500 | |
| Estimated tax 40% = £19,000 | | 19,000 |
| NET INCOME — AFTER TAX | | 46,400 |

**Note**

| | | £ |
|---|---|---|
| 1 Tax allowance 10% of fittings | = | 6,500 |
| 4% of buildings | = | 9,400 |
| | | 15,900 |

2 The continental breakfast would make the price very attactive, as competitors did not include it.

3 The additional income brought to the hotel by the above visitors in the bars and restaurant has *not* been included.

**Summary**

The extensions are still in the process of being built.

## 4   Self assessment questions

After working through the study material and text books test your knowledge.

1  What general factors are considered in working out a pricing policy?
2  What psychological factors influence the attitude of buyers to price?
3  Describe the pricing objectives of a catering unit.

## 5   Test VI

1  Why should cost-plus pricing be regarded as only a starting point to price setting?
2  What are the main advantages of using differential profit margins in a restaurant?
3  For what reasons is a hotel likely to use a variable price policy?

# VII
# Profit Planning

**Areas of study**
1  Advantages of profit planning
2  Budgetary control and a profit plan

**Objectives**
On completing this chapter and activities the reader should be able to:

(a)  describe how profit targets are set for accommodation and food departments
(b)  analyse the relationship between budgetary control and profit planning

**Activities**
1  A case study — preparation of profit plans
2  Self-assessment questions
3  Test VII
4  Multiple choice questions on marketing planning

**Readings**
GILES, *Marketing*, Chapter VIII

A market plan determines the course of the operation towards the most suitable markets and the most effective way of organising resources. The plan will include several objectives, but the fundamental objective is to make a profit, and as profits come from sales, it is usually the responsibility of the marketing manager.

## 1 Advantages of profit planning

(a) activities within the operation can be adjusted to achieve the most desired profit levels
(b) the profit plans can include a target element making management look ahead rather than at past results
(c) it provides objectives which are fundamental to the operation
(d) it encourages analysis and planning to react to the environmental changes rather than act in a crisis

Successful profit planning can only succeed if it is linked with budgetary control, and we should now see how this technique can be used.

## 2 Budgetary control and a profit plan

Budgetary control is a technique which forms an important part of a marketing management system.

It consists of planning profit objectives for the forthcoming trading period, usually one year, and subsequently comparing actual results, as they become known, with planned results.

The aims of budgetary control are:

(a) to ensure the best possible use of the resources of the business in obtaining maximum profitability
(b) to ensure that expenditure is within income
(c) to plan future action in detail and regulate the progress of the business
(d) to achieve co-ordination of all activities
(e) to establish clear lines of responsibility for each aspect of the business.

The control arises in two ways:
(i) by assigning responsibility for the achievement of the planned results to the appropriate manager
(ii) by taking appropriate action when variances from the budgets are observed

The usual period in hotels for which budgets are drawn up is twelve months. The comparison of actual results with planned results is carried out usually monthly or every four weeks. Clearly, the initial plan for each department must be concerned with sales targets, for it is from sales that the income is derived and the level of sales will affect all these costs, which vary with sales activity.

## THE FRAMEWORK OF BUDGETARY CONTROL
### For the Next FINANCIAL YEAR

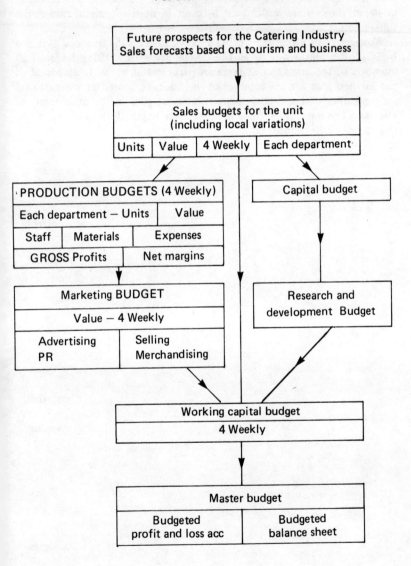

As the basic reasons for operating a system of budgetary control are the planning of profit objectives, and the monitoring of progress towards these objectives, budget preparation includes the drafting of profit and loss accounts for each operating department.

Budgetary control should be brought into use as a technique which is of proven value in clarifying the process of planning ahead, and in revealing in detail those areas which will be most in need of careful managerial supervision.

Management's attention is being directed towards the financial nuts and bolts of the business and, at the crucial stage of drafting budgets, all members of the management team are participating in the development of the forward plan for the conduct of the business. Moreover, the part that each member of the management team must play in the attainment of sales and the control of costs is made more explicitly by this technique than by any other approach.

In the hotel and catering industry, separate budgets are produced for the food, beverage and accommodation departments on a unit and value basis. The budgets are divided into four weekly periods and show by units and value the budgeted figures and the actual results as they become available.

## 1 Preparation of profit plans — case study — The Chiltern Hotel

Chapter III contained a case study which described the feasibility study and purchase of The Chiltern Hotel. The following pages continue with the case to:

(i) describe how the accounting procedures were changed, and provide better information for marketing decisions
(ii) show the construction of profit plans
(iii) involve the reader in calculations which will develop knowledge and understanding of profit planning.

### Changes to the present accounting procedures

Changes to the accounting procedures were suggested because the hotel management would benefit by having:

(a) the comparative profitabilities of the various departments
(b) information presented in such a way that management action to investigate and correct adverse results is facilitated
(c) a system of profit planning and control based upon drawing up future plans against which to measure progress and take necessary corrective action.

The present system of historical accounting has the merit of being relatively simple to implement and it fulfils legal requirements as to accounting records. But the hotel operations embrace three different activities within the one organisation, namely the provision of accommodation, food and beverage.

The assessment of profitability for each of these operations can only be accomplished by an allocation of expenses to each activity on a reasonable and consistent basis.

An important area of management accounting is the observation and interpretation of cost behaviour at varying levels of business activity. Before this can be done, it is generally necessary to classify costs into those costs which are fixed regardless of the level of activity, and those which vary in accordance with activity levels. One benefit from using this approach is the indication which it gives of the business which must be done to cover fixed costs, total costs, and to arrive at profit objectives.

### Profit plans for 1982

1 *Market research* The competitor's analysis and management forecasts
suggest that £12.25 per night be charged, including breakfast valued at
£1.00 and this would give a 45.33% sleeper occupancy of the 24 double
rooms.

The hotel closes for 15 days at Christmas.

Therefore a sleeper occuapncy of 45.33% for 350 days at £11.25 (bed
only) would produce sales of:

$$\frac{48}{1} \times \frac{45.33\%}{100} \times \frac{350}{1} \times \frac{11.25}{1} = £85,680$$

2 Food costs would be controlled at 40%, and sales of food would increase
in value by 10%
3 Beverage costs would be controlled at 50%, and sales of beverage would
increase in value by 10%

### The profit plan for 1982 (based on 1981 results)

|  | Rooms £ | Food £ | Beverage £ | Total £ |
|---|---|---|---|---|
| Sales | 85,680 | 42,500 | 25,000 | 153,180 |
| Less cost of goods sold | — | 17,000 | 12,500 | 29,500 |
| **Departmental gross profits** | 85,680 | 25,500 | 12,500 | 123,680 |
| Less wages and staff costs | 17,000 | 17,500 | 4,000 | 38,500 |
| **Net margin** | 68,680 | 8,000 | 8,500 | 85,180 |
| Less — allocated expenses | | | | |
| Fuel, cleaning, repairs | | | | |
| Depreciation, rates, etc, based on | | | | |
| invoice analysis plus 10% cost | | | | |
| increase | 14,400 | 5,000 | 1,700 | 21,100 |
| | 54,280 | 3,000 | 6,800 | 64,080 |

| | |
|---|---|
| **Less general and administration expenses (less items incorrectly charged last year)** | 25,580 |
| **Net profit before tax** | 38,500 |
| **Less — estimated tax — 50%** | 19,250 |
| **Net profit after tax** | 19,250 |

**The profit plan — accommodation**

Market research, the competitor's analysis and management's forecasts suggest that £12.25 per night be charged including breakfast valued at £1.00 and this would give a 45.33% occupancy. (The hotel closes for 15 days at Christmas.)

Therefore a sleeper occupancy of 45.33% for 350 days at £11.25 (bed only) would produce sales of:

$$= \frac{45.33}{100} \times \frac{350}{1} \times \frac{11.25}{1}$$

£
85,680

Total operating and administration expenses (fixed cost) for 1981:

|  | £ |  |
|---|---|---|
| Wages, staff | 38,500 | |
| Operating expenses | 21,100 | |
| *Administration expenses | 25,580 | |
|  | 85,180 | |
| LESS | | |
| Operating expenses/wages | | |
| absorbed by food | 22,500 | |
| absorbed by beverage | 5,700 | |
|  | 28,200 | 56,980 |
| Accommodation profit at 45.33% sleeper occupancy | | 28,700 |

| | |
|---|---|
| (a)  Calculate the percentage sleeper occupancy to break even | |
| (b)  Calculate the profit at 50% sleeper occupancy | |

*All administration expenses have been charged to rooms — the main reason being that the hotel exists because of the accommodation area.

**The profit plan — food and beverages**
It was decided that the restaurant and bar would be under the control of a
manager who would be responsible to the general manager.

A profit plan was made out after considering:

(a)  the average spending power of the present customers (£4)
(b)  the number of covers per year

| Estimated trading results | | | | |
|---|---|---|---|---|
| Description | Food | | Beverage | |
| | £ | % | £ | % |
| Sales (estimated) | 42,500 | 100 | 25,000 | 100 |
| Less food and bar costs | 17,000 | 40 | 12,500 | 50 |
| Less staff | 17,500 | 41 | 4,000 | 16 |
| Less Expenses | 5,000 | 12 | 1,700 | 7 |
| Dept profit margins | 3,000 | 7 | 6,800 | 27 |

| Food Sales — differential profit margins | | | | |
|---|---|---|---|---|
| Sales mix | % | £ | DPM | £ |
| Soup/appetisers | 15 | 6,375 | 75 | 4,780 |
| Meat/Fish | 40 | 17,000 | 50 | 8,500 |
| Vegetables | 20 | 8,500 | 70 | 5,950 |
| Sweets | 20 | 8,500 | 55 | 4,690 |
| Tea/Coffee | 5 | 2,125 | 75 | 1,580 |
| Gross profit | 100 | 42,500 | 60 | 25,500 |

1  Calculate the expected profit if food and beverage sales are increased
   by 10%
2  Design a differential profit plan for the beverage sales. The sales mix
   is estimated to be:

|  | £ |
|---|---|
| Minerals | 1,000 |
| Beers | 8,000 |
| Table wines | 7,000 |
| Fortified wines | 3,000 |
| Spirits | 6,000 |
|  | 25,000 |

## 2   Self assessment questions

After working through the study material and text books, test your knowledge:

1  What is budgetary control?
2  Describe the links between budgetary control, the sales budget, and proft planning.

## 3   Test VII

1  Describe the advantages of profit planning for a hotel or restaurant.
2  Describe and evaluate the main factors in constructing a sales budget.
3  State the purpose of budgetary control and discuss the factors to be considered in relation to business forecasting for a hotel.

**Multiple choice questions on marketing planning**
From the following statements choose what you consider to be the correct answers:

1  Marketing planning seeks mainly to:
(a)  determine the products to be sold and methods of distribution to use
(b)  estimate the level of profit required, and develop a sales programme to reach the required level
(c)  forecast the sales and costs for the next year and adjust last year's plan accordingly
(d)  determine the course of business towards suitable markets and organise resources accordingly.

2  The first stage of product planning is to:
(a)  determine the priorities of the company
(b)  measure past performances
(c)  identify current need and wants
(d)  determine costs
(e)  analyse competitors' activities.

3  The first stage of a promotion campaign is to:
(a)  identify the best media to use
(b)  formulate the messages
(c)  determine what needs to be sold
(d)  calculate the costs
(e)  select the market segments to be reached.

4  A restaurant wants to set an average selling price so that it provides a profit for the year of £10,000. Estimated sales are 20,000 covers. Fixed costs are £10,000, and variable costs £2 per cover. What should the selling price be.
(a)  £3,  (b)  £5,  (c)  £7,  (d)  £2,  (e)  £4

# VIII
# Marketing Control

**Areas of study**
1 Performance evaluation
2 Budgetary control and variance analysis
3 Customer satisfaction rates

**Objectives**
On completing this chapter and activities the reader should be able to:
(a) describe the marketing control techniques in the hotel and catering industry
(b) explain how marketing variances are analysed

**Activities**
1 Multiple choice questions on marketing control
2 Self-assessment questions
3 Test VIII

**Readings**
GILES, *Marketing*, Chapter VIII

The marketing plan highlights the objectives to be attained and the methods of operation during a particular time, but throughout the particular period it is necessary to check the correct performance against the standards set within the plan. This will establish whether any corrective action is necessary to ensure that the desired results and actual performance are as near as possible.

It follows that management and staff must know:

1  the objectives to be attained
2  the performance achieved, perodically during the year
3  the variations, reasons and causes, in order to implement corrective action.

## 1  Performance evaluation

Performance evaluation is necessary because there are so many variable factors and unexpected events that can take place during a financial year, such as:

(a)  plans may turn out to be unrealistic, because of hidden ambiguities, and management will wish to reappriase their forecasts and plans
(b)  competitors' activities may alter the supply and demand position and management will wish to react to the changed situation
(c)  environmental and social changes may take place altering the expected performance of the unit.

It is important that management is made aware of the implications of change, and preplanned review meetings should be held, usually every four weeks, so as to give an aopportunity for managers and supervisors to present reasons for failing to achieve targets and standards of performance. This means that an information system must operate.

### Marketing information system
A manager or section head needs a reliable marketing information system which will help in:

(a)  the setting of standards, often from past performances
(b)  monitoring of results against standards
(c)  communicating, to the staff concerned, the areas needing attention and feeding back the action taken.

*A Marketing control system*

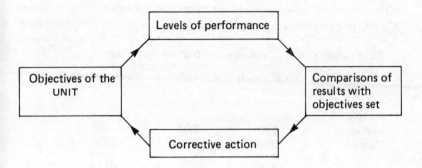

Control in marketing management for the hotel and catering industry is measured by financial and statistical results and is related to:

(a) revenue producing area of:
    food
    beverage
    accommodation
(b) the promotional activities.

## Marketing control and the link with budgetary control

A budgetary control system has been mentioned and described in the planning section, as a method which establishes objectives for the forthcoming period, usually one year, and subsequently compares actual results, as they become known.

The control arises in two ways:

1 by assigning responsibility for the objectives set
2 by seeing that appropriate action is taken when variances from the budget are observed

## 2 Budgetary control and variance analysis

As the marketing manager places more emphasis on profit than on sales turnover, he needs to be aware of the factors under his control, which fluctuate and cause variation in the expected profits, such as:

(a) prices
(b) total volume of sales
(c) average spend per customer.

The budgetary control system can provide comparisons between planned and actual results in the following form.

123

**Note**

Costs of services and products have not been included in these variances as they are beyond the control of the marketing manager.

**A marketing variance analysis statement**

Food variance analysis statement — four weeks ending . . . . . . .

|   |   | No of covers | ASP £ | Sales turnover £ |
|---|---|---|---|---|
| **1** | **Budget** | | | |
| | Lunches | 450 | 2.00 | 900 |
| | Dinners | 900 | 6.00 | 5400 |
| | | 1350 | | 6300 |
| **2** | **Actual** | | | |
| | Lunches | 500 | 1.80 | 900 |
| | Dinners | 750 | 7.00 | 5250 |
| | | 1250 | | 6150 |

The statement above shows that sales turnover has fallen slightly, but by analysing the sales variances, volume and price, a marketing manager is able to explain in detail, the cost to the firm.

**Note**

A variance is said to be adverse if it works against the company, and is favourable if it works for the company.

1  The *total sales variance* represents the difference between total budgeted and total actual sales.

   In this case an adverse variance of
   £6300 - £6150 = £150 (A)

2  Volume variance — we find the difference between the budgeted and the actual customers and multiply by the budgeted ASP.
   This factor by itself would have caused an adverse variance of £800

|   | Number of covers | | | Budget Price | Lunches £ | Dinners £ |
|---|---|---|---|---|---|---|
| | **Budget** | **Actual** | **Difference** | | | |
| Lunches | 450 | 500 | + 50 | 2.00 = | 100 (F) | |
| Dinners | 900 | 750 | - 150 | 6.00 = | | - 900(A) |

3 *Average spending power variance* shows the effect on total sales if the amount of money spent varies from the budgeted figures.

| | Prices | | | Actual | | |
|---|---|---|---|---|---|---|
| | Budget £ | Actual £ | Difference £ | sales | Lunches £ | Dinners £ |
| Lunches | 2.00 | 1.80 | − 0.20 | 500 = | − 100(A) | |
| Dinners | 6.00 | 7.00 | + 1.00 | 750 = | | + 750(F) |

The variances can now be collected to explain the total variance.

| | Lunch £ | Dinners £ |
|---|---|---|
| Volume variance (2) | 100 (F) | 900(A) |
| ASP/price variance (3) | 100 (A) | 750(F) |
| Total variance (1) | NIL | 150(A) |

With the aid of these variances the marketing manager knows where to concentrate his efforts in maintaining favourable variances, and preventing adverse variances in the future. In the example above:

(a) the menu popularity index could identify the types of meals and drinks ordered which is giving an ASP of £7 rather than the expected £6

(b) the variances show an increase in customers at lunch-time and a decrease in the evening. This fluctuation could have been hidden if all the statistics had been collected and not analysed.

**Ratio analysis**
The technique of ratio analysis is useful for control purposes for it can measure:

(a) degrees of efficiency
(b) levels of activity
(c) use of resources.

These measures can then be used to help a marketing manager follow trends within his business and compare his results with other units within the same company, or general ratios presented by a trade association.

The ratios are often produced and presented with other statistical information and shown on a marketing operational statement. An example is shown overleaf.

A marketing operational control statement

Period — four weeks ending

| Bedrooms | Budget | Actual | Remarks |
|---|---|---|---|
| 1 Percentage of rooms occupied | | | |
| 2 Percentage of beds occupied | | | |
| 3 Average room rate | | | |
| 4 Average spend per guest | | | |
| 5 Average length of stay | | | |
| | | | |
| Function rooms | | | |
| 1 Occupancy percentage | | | |
| 2 Number of functions | | | |
| 3 Average spend on food | | | |
| 4 Average spend on drink | | | |
| | | | |
| Food | | | |
| 1 No of covers — Lunch | | | |
| 2 No of covers — Evening | | | |
| 3 Average spend | | | |
| 4 percentage food cost to sales | | | |
| 5 percentage gross profit | | | |
| 6 Drink sales per cover | | | |
| | | | |
| Beverages | | | |
| Sales of spirits — £s | | | |
| Sales of wine — £s | | | |
| Sales of beer — £s | | | |
| Sales of other — £s | | | |
| % Drink cost ot sales | | | |
| % Gross profit | | | |
| Stock turnover on wine | | | |
| Stock turnover on spirits | | | |

These statistics show up variations within a four-weekly period and can be compared with previous periods to show trends.

## Inter-firm comparison

The University of Strathclyde collects hotel comparative data and firms in the industry are able to compare their own performance against other firms. The comparisons measure the managerial effectiveness of using resources. There are some limitations in using these figures, and they should be taken only as a guide. This subject is dealt with in greater detail in the management accountancy field of study.

# 3 Customer satisfaction rates

Financial results will show the progress a catering unit is making towards reaching its financial objectives, but the success of any catering firm will depend on the level of customer satisfaction, as it is known that a satisfied customer:

(a) will return, and
(b) provide the most effective form of advertising, by word of mouth!

For example in the 1970s customer surveys showed the displeasure the visitors to Malta, expressed about dirty beaches, and this was quickly tackled by the Maltese Government and corrected. A hotel group analysed their customer reactions to their hotels in the Mediterranean and were able to identify problems in some hotels and correct them to the mutual benefit of the company and customer.

(a) In one hotel only 47% of the customers staying at the hotel were satisfied with the food. As this was an unusually low percentage it was investigated and it was found that food portions were far too small.
(b) In another hotel a low service rating of 49% showed up the speed of service as being at fault.

In both instances the faults were corrected, and now the hotels are operating at the same levels as the others in the group — approximately 75%.

### New plans for the restaurant at The Chiltern Hotel

After The Chiltern Hotel had been operating under the new management the control system showed the reataurant sales to be very disappointing. Statistics showed the following trend:

| | Quarter | Sales £ | |
|---|---|---|---|
| 1980/81 | Nov to Jan | 9,910 | |
| | Feb to April | 10,060 | |
| | May to July | 9,840 | |
| | Aug to Oct | 8,890 | |
| | Nov to Jan | 8,800 | |
| 1982 | Feb to April | 8,600 | Under new management |

(a) Work out the percentage decrease compared with the same period last year

(b) Calculate the average of covers served each day if the ASP was £4.00

```

```

(c) Design a questionnaire to determine satisfaction levels of guests and customers using the hotel.

# Activities

## 1  Multiple choice questions on marketing control

From the following statements choose what you consider to be the correct answers:

1  The factors under the control of a marketing manager would not include:
(a)  prices of products and services
(b)  cost of products and services
(c)  the total volume of sales
(d)  the average spending power of customers.

2  Which of the following statements comes closest to being correct?
(a)  Marketing control is essential to keep prices stable
(b)  Control arises by seeing that appropriate action is taken when variances from the budget are observed
(c)  Marketing control is essential to stop over expenditure on materials and labour
(d)  Control provides statistical information for forecasting and planning.

3  Ratio analysis measures the following factors, except:
(a)  degrees of efficiency
(b)  levels of activity
(c)  use of resources
(d)  the cost of operations.

4  Which statement is correct?
(a)  Budgetary control helps to plan future action and regulate the progress of the business
(b)  Budgetary control is used to allocate revenue and capital expenditure.
(c)  Budgetary control is an accounting technique for control purposes.

## 2 Self assessment questions

After working through the study material and text books, test your knowledge:

1 What is the function of marketing control?
2 Has inter-firm comparison anything to offer marketing management?
3 Explain the nature and purpose of using budgets?

## 3 Test VIII

1 Food and beverage variance analysis statement — four weeks' ending. . . .

|  |  | No of covers | ASP | Sales turnover |
|---|---|---|---|---|
| (A) | **Budget** |  |  | £ |
|  | Lunches | 300 | 2.0 | 600 |
|  | Dinners | 150 | 5.0 | 750 |
|  |  | 450 |  | 1350 |
| (B) | **Actual** |  |  |  |
|  | Lunches | 300 | 2.0 | 600 |
|  | Dinner | 100 | 6.0 | 600 |
|  |  | 400 |  | 1200 |

Analyse the variances and write a report to the general manager

2 As marketing manager, which ratios would you consider to be most helpful?

The two main objectives of an hotel were to achieve:

1 a high rate of customer satisfaction
2 a good return on capital invested.

The profit plan showed that a satisfactory result could be expected, provided certain intended conditions are kept. It would be the manager's task to check constantly to see that results during the year are in line with the objectives set out within the marketing plan.

A control system was introduced to show:

(a) objective and standards in quantitative form
(b) a knowledge of progress made
(c) a comparison of objectives and progress to date
(d) a method of correcting action, of operational results are unsatisfactory.

129

---

**Exercise**

Write a report showing what information should be provided for a hotel manager, differentiating between financial and operating statistics and showing:

(a) the frequency of presentation

(b) sources and methods of collection

---

# An Integrated Case Study
# —The Whitegate Hotel,
# Chester

**An integrated case study**
The following case study covers the challenges and opportunities presented
to an hotel manager in the county of Cheshire. It is hoped that by analysing
the data, the students will develop their knowledge and understanding of
marketing within the hotel and catering industry, and prepare themselves
in a practical way for marketing management and the future.

**Introduction**
The Whitegate Hotel, Chester, is a Cambrian hotel situated at Buddington
some seven miles away from the city centre. It is strategically located close
to the M56 which links with Manchester Airport, the M6 and M63 which
links up with the M62. It is, therefore, readily accessible to people who
want to travel to the north, south, east or west of the country, and since
there is a regular bus service to and from the city centre which runs past
the hotel, it is also easily accessible to Chester city centre.

The hotel itself has been open for five years and offers numerous
facilities especially for the businessman. These include 201 double bedrooms with modern facilities such as private bathroom, television and
radio; a large banqueting suite which can be subdivided into four sections;
an hospitality and ten syndicate rooms, and ample parking space for 240
cars. Conference facilities are available on a residential or daily rate and
there is a restaurant which is open for lunch and dinners; a buttery for
breakfast and snacks which is open until 11.00 pm; and two bars.

Within the immediate vicinity of the hotel there are no other large
hotels although as one moves nearer towards Chester city centre, the
number of hotels increases, many of which also offer business and
conference facilities. The main competition for the hotel, therefore, lies
in its easy access to the town and from hotels situated in Helsby, Wrexham
and Whiteway. Although two speciality restaurants have opened within
three miles of the hotel during the last two years, they are not thought to
be a threat.

During the week the main trade is from businessmen who can take
advantage of the accessibility and conference facilities, but during the
week-end it is from families who can take advantage of the Bargain Break
week-ends offered by the company, and the family bedrooms which can
accommodate parents with one or two children.

The present manager of the hotel, Mr Pugh, has been with the hotel for 3½ years and during this time has increased the sleeper occupancy level from 52.4% to 73.9%, and the sales from £million to £1.6 million. The main restaurant of the hotel has been operating since the hotel was built, for seven days a week and since it has now reached the mature stage of its product life cycle, the manager has decided to bring about a change because the number of customers have been declining.

### The restaurant before November 1978

Over the past five years the county restaurant has been operating without a change except in the case of the menu which is automatically altered every six months, for seven nights a week. It is a medium-sized restaurant with a maximum capacity of 82 covers, the take-up level of which had been falling. The staff consist of a restaurant manager, his deputy — who is mainly concerned with wine sales; two Chefs de Rang, two Commis' and five waitresses. In the evenings a cashier and hostess are also employed, the latter having the job of selling the various services offered and taking orders.

From Monday through to Friday a table d'hote and the full à la carte menu were offered for lunch. Special company promotion dishes, such as steak and scampi platters, were also available. In the evening there was a chef's choice and the full à la carte menu. In addition to this if the customer has a special request then the chef would do his best to comply with it. This service was not advertised on the menu, however!

The prices of the various menus were as follows:

| | |
|---|---|
| Table d'hote lunch | £3.50 |
| A la carte | £5.40 without wine |
| Company promotion Platters | £3.95 |
| Chef's Choice | £5.75 |

Prices have been increased by 15% a year for the last three years.

On Saturday the morning was reserved for food and personal hygiene training of restaurant staff; and the afternoon for wedding receptions. On such occasions the maximum capacity for a sit-down lunch was 80 people.

On Sunday a special lunch was offered at a fixed price of £2.95 adults and £2.50 for children, in the evening a limited à la carte menu.

A wide range of wines was available with both lunch and dinner, throughout the week.

Within the kitchen it was the hotel's policy to use no frozen foods except in the case of such items as scampi or fruit that was out of season. The vegetables and fruit were brought every two days and cooked fresh.

With regard to the decoration of the restaurant, the main colour scheme was purple, the walls being aubergine and purple and the floor being covered with an aubergine, purple and orange carpet of a circular design. The windows were covered with heavy pink net curtains, and dark purple, straight hung drapes. The colour theme was carried through to the tables and chairs, the former being covered with pink tablecloths and the latter being painted purple.

The menu consisted of a buff folding card contained within a wine coloured leather folder. The choice was fairly extensive with appetisers, soups, fish and farinaceous dishes, meat and poultry dishes, Italian specialities, dishes cooked at the table and from the Flare Grill being offered along with a variety of vegetables and salads, sweets and coffee.

Stock levels at the end of the year were as follows:

|  | Food £ | Beverages £ |
|---|---|---|
| 1975 | 720 | 1200 |
| 1976 | 780 | 1600 |
| 1977 | 880 | 2200 |
| 1978 | 980 | 4200 |

**Financial analysis details — Last four weeks of 1978**
The last four weeks of 1978 produced the following financial statistics compared with the budget figures.

|  |  | Actual | Budget |
|---|---|---|---|
| Number of covers | — Dinners | 825 | 1,000 |
|  | — Lunches | 450 | 500 |
| ASP | Dinners | £6.00 | £6.75 |
|  | Lunches | £4.25 | £4.00 |

**Statistical analysis — six months ending 1978**

|  | Lunch | Evening |
|---|---|---|
| Hours opened each day | 3 | 5 |
| Number of covers sold | 3,500 | 7,000 |

The concern expressed by the hotel manager of the reducing numbers using the restaurant resulted in the directors seeking the assistance of a marketing consultant. A summary of his report is presented below.

**Report from a marketing consultant**

**Objective**
To determine the reasons why the number of customers using the hotel restaurant was decreasing.

The financial results of the restaurant are shown below:

**Lunch and dinners only**

**Operating statements – years ending 31 December**

|  |  | 1976 |
|---|---|---|
| Sales: Food | 72000 | |
| Beverage | 30000 | |
| | ——— | 102000 |
| Less: cost of sales: food | 28800 | |
| beverage | 15000 | |
| | ——— | 43800 |
| GROSS MARGIN | | 58200 |
| Less: wages and staff expenses | | 28050 |
| NET MARGIN | | 30150 |
| Less: heat, light and power | 9180 | |
| Advertising | 2040 | |
| Administration | 5100 | |
| General operating expense | 2550 | |
| Rent, rates and insurance | 1250 | |
| Repairs and renewals | 1000 | |
| Depreciation | 750 | |
| Financial expenses | 1000 | |
| | ——— | 22870 |
| | | 7280 |

| 1977 | | 1978 | |
|---|---|---|---|
| 78000 | | 86000 | |
| 30000 | | 37000 | |
| ——— | 111000 | ——— | 123000 |
| 33540 | | 38700 | |
| 17160 | | 20350 | |
| ——— | 50700 | ——— | 59050 |
| | 60300 | | 63950 |
| | 32190 | | 37515 |
| | 28110 | | 26435 |
| 10545 | | 12300 | |
| 2250 | | 2500 | |
| 6660 | | 8000 | |
| 2650 | | 2750 | |
| 1300 | | 1400 | |
| 1100 | | 1100 | |
| 750 | | 750 | |
| 1000 | | 1000 | |
| ——— | 26255 | ——— | 29800 |
| | 1855 | | (3365) |

**Procedure**

A restaurant is chosen partly because of its functional qualities, the ability to serve good food and partly to satisfy psychological attributes. It was therefore decided to determine which factors influencing a persons choice were not being satisfied by the hotel restaurant.

A questionnaire was designed, and two hundred people were interviewed and asked to rate factors of preference against a scale A to E, with A being the most important when choosing a restaurant in the evening. The results are summarised below:

**Ranking**

1 Quality and type of food
2 Atmosphere
3 Licensed premises
4 Price
5 Efficiency of management and staff
6 Promotional messages
7 Location
8 Speed of service
9 Cleanliness

A second questionnaire was designed featuring similar factors to the general survey, to establish if any correlation occurred between the general public and customers using the hotel restaurant and the two competing restaurants within three miles of the hotel.

The respondents for the second questionnaire were asked to list those factors that they related and associated with the units being analysed, by multi-attribute attitude measures.

The results are shown below:

| Factor | Hotel Rest | Restaurant A | Restaurant B |
|---|---|---|---|
| 1 Quality and type of food | 5.16 | 5.20 | 5.14 |
| 2 Atmosphere | 2.80 | 4.86 | 4.90 |
| 3 Price (good value for money) | 4.90 | 4.70 | 4.56 |
| 4 Efficiency of management and staff | 4.80 | 4.60 | 4.65 |
| 5 Speed of service | 3.80 | 4.20 | 4.15 |
| 6 Cleanliness | 3.15 | 4.15 | 4.35 |

**Note**

Licensed premises and promotional messages and location not included as they were considered to the same for this inquiry.

The results highlighted how the restaurants were perceived in the public's mind and pinpointed the weaknesses that needed managerial attention.

**Relevant statistics**

**TABLE 1  Sleeper occupancy**

|  | 1977 | 1978 |
|---|---|---|
| First quarter | 58.0% | 55.9% |
| Second quarter | 76.0% | 86.6% |
| Third quarter | 86.0% | 92.6% |
| Fourth quarter | 59.0% | 56.9% |
| Weighted average | 69.0% | 73.9% |

**TABLE 2  Breakdown of business**

|  | 1977 | 1978 |
|---|---|---|
| Business executive | 58.0 | 55.0 |
| Inclusive tours (including week-end breaks) | 10.0 | 13.0 |
| Foreign tourist (Independent) | 10.0 | 20.0 |
| Groups/conferences | 22.0 | 12.0 |
|  | 100% | 100% |

**TABLE 3  Guest — country of origin**

|  | 1977 % | 1978 % |
|---|---|---|
| United Kingdom | 71 | 70 |
| EEC | 6 | 16 |
| North America | 12 | 3 |
| Others | 11 | 11 |
|  | 100 | 100 |

**Answer the following:**

1 Faced with the situation described, how would you, as the newly-appointed general manager of the Whitegate Hotel, determine the problems and opportunities facing you, and how would you set about dealing with them?

2 Analyse the financial operating statement and, together with other data available, highlight important changes that have taken place over the last years.

# Sample questions from HCIMA examination papers

## MARKETING 1

**Question 1**
Within the Hotel and Catering Industry:
(a) what contribution does market research make to the overall marketing plan? (10 marks)
(b) indicate the main sources of data (10 marks)

**Question 2**
Discuss what factors you would expect to be considered in a feasibility study by a company, before a decision is made to build a restaurant in a particular area?

**Question 3**
(a) What is the Product Life Cycle? (5 marks)
(b) How can an understanding of the concept of the Product Life Cycle be of use to management in the Hotel and Catering Industry? Give examples. (15 marks)

**Question 4**
'Anyone contemplating a business venture in one of the service industries must possess insights into man's needs to be able to devise the necessary satisfaction if he is to succeed' (Marketing the Meal Experience) (Campbell-Smith)
Outline the pattern of thought behind this statement with particular reference to the eating out situation.

**Question 5**
What information sources can you use to judge the popularity/effectiveness of your marketing strategy?

**Question 6**
What are the major applications for marketing control techniques within the hotel and catering industry?

**Question 7**
Explain and discuss the Marketing Concept. (12 marks)

139

How can this concept be applied in the catering services of
(a) hospitals
(b) schools? (8 marks)

## Question 8
Describe the type of promotional mix that may be used by a large hotel
company operating large luxury hotels. (10 marks)
Explain how you would identify the market areas at which to aim your
promotional campaign. (10 marks)

## Question 9
Describe the main environmental forces facing the hotel industry.

## Question 10
Indicate the main factors to be borne in mind prior to research
investigations. (5 marks)
Describe the main types of data and show how they may be applied to
areas of the hotel and catering industry. (15 marks)

## Question 11
Describe two of the following, and discuss their application in the hotel
and catering industry.
(a) Public Relations (10 marks)
(b) Customer Orientation (10 marks)
(c) Budgetary Control (10 marks)
(d) Market Segmentation (10 marks)

## Question 12
(a) What is a marketing plan and why is it important? (10 marks)
(b) Explain how you would procuce a 2 year marketing plan for a 50
bedroom hotel operating in the United Kingdom. (10 marks)

## Question 13
(a) Describe the difference between marketing and selling. (10 marks)
(b) Discuss the role that marketing can play within the hotel and
catering industry. (10 marks)

## Question 14
(a) What are the functions of marketing research? (5 marks)
(b) Describe the data you would expect a manager to use, before a
decision is made to develop a hotel in a particular area. (15 marks)

## Question 15
(a) List the methods which might be used in a Selling Campaign for a
hotel. (10 marks)
(b) Describe the characteristics and state the advantage of the methods
which you have listed. (10 marks)

## Question 16
Within the Hotel and Catering Industry:
(a) what contribution does market research make to the overall marketing plan? (10 marks)
(b) indicate the main sources of data. (10 marks)


## Question 17
You have been asked to carry out a 'Market Analysis' for your Hotel. Describe the basic principles which have to be applied when carrying out the analysis and the areas that would be included in your study. (20 marks)

## Question 18
(a) Advertising is an impersonal form of communication aimed essentially at persuading customers and potential customers to adopt a favourable attitude to an identified organisation, product or service.
On the basis of this definition, state the specific objectives that an advertising campaign for a Hotel may have, and suggest which types of advertising might be most appropriate. (10 marks)
(b) Discuss briefly the main ways of measuring the effectiveness of advertising. (10 marks)

## Question 19
Discuss the factors you would consider in setting prices within the catering industry. (20 marks)

## Question 20
'Customer orientation is fundamental to marketing thinking and policy.' Discuss this statement and its application to both profit and non-profit organisations. (20 marks)

# Index